THE PERSONALITY OF SEMINARIANS

A Study Guide and Reference Work

Vincent V. Herr, S.J.

Nihil Obstat:
Daniel V. Flynn, J.C.D.
Censor Librorum

Imprimatur:
Joseph P. O'Brien, S.T.D.
Vicar General, Archdiocese of New York
August 12, 1969

The nihil obstat and imprimatur are official declarations that a book or pamphlet is free of doctrinal or moral error. No implication is contained therein that those who have granted the nihil obstat and imprimatur agree with the contents, opinions or statements expressed.

Copyright 1970 by the Society of St. Paul, 2187 Victory Blvd., Staten Island, N.Y. 10314

Library of Congress Catalog Card Number. 72-94698
SBN. 8189-0168-3

Designed, printed and bound in the U.S.A. by the Pauline Fathers and Brothers, 2187 Victory Blvd., Staten Island, N.Y. 10314 as part of their communications apostolate.

FOREWORD*

This little treatise is designed for a twofold purpose. Firstly, it will tell the busy Guidance worker, the student personnel worker, or the student Counsellor at a glance, some of the leading contributions to the topic of the discrimination of college students from candidates for the priesthood and religious life. Secondly, it will present at least one theory of character and personality, which has been widely taught by professors and researchers in the fields of psychology and psychiatry. The definitions will be elaborated in chapter I.

The treatise is definitely not meant to be an exhaustive treatment of personality theory, as can be judged by its size. It is rather designed to present some tenable guidelines for building up one's own theory of character and personality. The concepts in chapter I are frankly eclectic. That is to say, they are borrowed from many sources, and some are more theoretical and a priori than empirical. There are avilable empirical foundations for most of the concepts also; that is so say, there is available a plethora of applied material, from the studies done on college students over a long period of time, that could support the theory which is predominant in chapter I. The theory is neither what

* This study is supported in part by the National Institute of Mental Health, Grant # 2M-6404.

would be called a "typological" one, nor one proper to the "trait psychologists" in modern and earlier psychology. By this is meant that behavioral traits come in for classification and identification in this treatise, as well as basic temperament types. This will be more true in chapter II, whereas in chapter I the dichotomy is between ego-centered traits and socio-centered ones. A sample test for self-diagnosis according to the concepts found in chapter I will be found in the Appendix.

A very special reason for including a definition of personality and character in chapter I is the fact that the notion of *normal* personality, is something which has confused writers for ages. Before we can hope to give clear notions of deviant forms of personality, we ought to be able to define the *normal* in very clear terms. If the author seems to labor the point of "normal function" of all the faculties, the reader will know that he is reacting to the tendency of many authors today, writing on the subject of character and personality; they simply dodge the issue of a clear and acceptable definition. This the author does not intend to do.

When one goes from chapter I to chapter II he will be introduced to a more complex theory or set of theories. The ones presented there have been perfected for many years in Canada and abroad. There will be given many empirical foundations for the eightfold classification of the temperaments, and the conceptual background is rather more a priori in this chapter then is that for chapter I. Again, in the Appendix will be found a self-diagnostic inventory, based upon the concepts found in chapter II. In chapter III, an advanced formulation will be found, based upon some concepts proper to the Minn. Multiphasic Personality Inventory. This chapter appeals very heavily to the actual studies that have been made using this inventory as a discriminatory tool for seminarians. Again the chapter, though empirically founded, is not by any means lacking in theoretical foundations, as is obvious from the history of the Minnesota Inventory.

In chapter IV there will be described a whole battery of tests which have been perfected at Loyola University over the years. This battery contains some very simple paper-and-pencil tests, which are found in the Appendix, and which can be self-scored; as well as other free-association tests in printed form; these latter have been fully standardized and are copyrighted. Therefore they must be sent to the Loyola Researchers for scoring and interpretation. Similarly the other tests of the battery will require the cooperation of competent psychologists, before any kind of meaningful interpretation can be given.

It should be repeated that the tests listed in the Appendix are for the purpose of understanding the text, rather than for making a meaningful self-diagnosis. The studies reported in chapter I are mostly of a purely commonsense type, and hence the tests in the Appendix are given so that the reader may understand the concepts contained in the chapter. Neither chapter I nor II is strictly either philosophical (theoretical) or empirical (validated through experience). There is more empirical evidence given for chapter IV than for any other. It would be a mistake to interpret the author's mind as if he were presenting some purely theoretical and some purely empirical findings. The four chapters are of a mixed and interrelated character, with empirical data, derived from the author's team of researchers, found more conspicuously in the last two chapters, the theoretical more in chapters I and II. By no means should the references to "religious" values in chapters II and III be taken to mean that a "theology" of character is presented. The orientation of the whole treatise is toward "reality as we find it" and by no means toward the verification of any theory whatsoever. Of course the general orientation of the work is that of a professing Christian.

This book is the result of thirty years of experience, teaching seminarians at a large western Seminary, and non-seminarians at a larger western university. The major interest throughout has been the assessment of personality, especially from the empirical, test-experimental point of view. This was the best way for the author to proceed, since he had been trained in Germany, the birthplace of the experimental method in psychology. The author had been sent there in order to study social psychology, and secured a degree in the Nazi-ruled Germany of Hitler days, after experiencing social tensions of all sorts first hand.

Many of the experimental techniques described in the present volume were acquired during those years in Germany. This may seem somewhat enigmatical to those who know what happened to the science of psychology during those days. Actually most of the author's studies had been finished in pre-Nazi Vienna under the famous Karl and Charlotte Buehler. The remainder was in the Rhineland, and those who know history will appreciate the fact that not much Nazi influence was visible in pre-war Bonn University. The people of the Rhineland resembled those in other parts of the south very little in those days. Hence, the author's research would be completed in true empirical fashion in spite of socialist rule, not because of it. The topic for doctoral research was the relation between perception and personality traits. Thus the experiences in Europe were quite helpful for the present study.

One of the researches reported in this book used 50 seminarians and 50 college students. Let it be recalled, that every one of the tests used in the battery had been validated upon hundreds of college students, and literally thousands of seminarians in and around the Chicago area. Hence there will be nothing to fear in regard to the adequacy of the sample used in the research project. Currently some of the tests are being replicated in various schools in other parts of the country.

The original research was supported by a ten-year grant from the National Institute of Mental Health. Each test report in the book gives due credit to this source. Without the help of the Institute the survey and subsequent test battery would not have been possible.

It is perfectly in line with the wishes of our Holy Father, as well as of the members of Vatican II, that such an investigation be made. In fact, the post-conciliar commission on Seminary training specifically recommends it. The Loyola researchers have been keeping in close touch with a bishop on this commission, and who promises to consider the findings in his own recommendations. This ardent supporter of the Loyola Project is none other than his Excellency, Bishop Ernest J. Primeau, bishop of Manchester, New Hampshire, who has written the preface to this book. He is actively cooperating with another of Loyola's Projects, namely the Mental Health Training of Seminarians. This is a multi-faith project and at the time of this writing, Yeshiva University is the principal school engaged in the cooperative study, under the aspects of a larger U.S. Health supported Project on Marriage and the Family. The Yeshiva Project is under the leadership of Rabbi I. Fred Hollander, Chief of the New York Board of Rabbis, and one who has been very active in ecumenical circles. Harvard University is also actively represented in the study of the Mental Health Training in our seminaries; this protestant phase of the project is under the directorship of the Dean of the Harvard Divinity School, Very Reverend Samuel H. Miller, D.D.

One might go on mentioning agencies, which in recent days have become deeply concerned, not only with preserving and bettering the mental health of our ministers and their parishioners, but also in trying to resolve the problems that often arise, when medical treatment policies come into conflict with the recommendations of churchmen. Thus the outcome of such studies may be expected to yield, not only an improvement in the health of all concerned, but also a more wide-spread prevention of mental illnesses, which seem to be so noticeably on the increase in recent times.

PREFACE

It gives me great pleasure to write the preface for this small volume on "The Personality of Seminarians." It represents the results of long years of study and painstaking research, on the part of the author, as well as of the many collaborators mentioned in the acknowledgments. I have been personally in contact with the author and can speak with some authority on his work and its implications for the future of seminarians all over the world. He, along with his associates, have written two other books, both published by Alba House, an international publications firm. One of them is in collaboration with a psychiatrist and is entitled, "Psychodynamics of Personality Development"; the other was produced with the close cooperation of graduate students and is entitled, "Religious Psychology."Both of these are being translated into several foreign languages, due largely to the efforts of the Editor of Alba House, in Staten Island, New York.

The volume on Personality deals with the all important topic of selection of candidates for the priesthood and for the religious life. It is directed mostly to student counsellors and workers in the field of personnel selection and guidance, though the general reader can do well to glance at the first three chapters, so that he may see some of the trends that are taking place in the assessment of religious vocations today. The several chapters progress from the more simple topics to the more complex. Thus it is only the more sophisticated reader who is likely to be able to gain the full benefit from reading the research orientated portions of the book.

This might really be an asset rather than a limitation, since it is not to be expected that the person with little or no training in psychology would be able to interpret the statistics involved in the evaluation of the various tests. In chapters I, II, and III there is a minimum of technical terminology used, and the lay reader may well profit by the discussion of the several simple personality tests described there; samples of some of these tests will be found at the end of the book.

If the present writer were to be asked which part of the book deserves highest approval by the public generally, he would probably wish to say that it would be chapter II. The tests here described are straightforward, and will remind the reader very powerfully of the ancient Greeks and their system of relating temperament traits to body types.

There follows a brief description of the content of the book. There are in chapter I some basic concepts of personality, temperament and character. Then the author gives some sample test questions that have been widely used for identifying traits that have to do with estimating a person's sense of self-worth on the one hand, and his sense of group or social belonging on the other.

In chapter II there are eight temperament types described. These can be found among any large group of persons, and each is in some degree different, but also to a large degree similar to those of the other seven types. A simple question-answer inventory is presented and this allows of an estimate of such basic types or trait tendencies as have been written about from the time of Hippocrates. These are, in a scaled order with the more desirable ones in the middle, and taking the criterion of desirability as goodness or weakness of the person's adjustment; 1. the amorphous; 2. the passionate; 3. the apathetic; 4. the choleric; 5. the sanguine; 6. the sentimental; 7. the phlegmatic; 8. the nervous. The amorphous type will be rather reserved, calm, submissive and passive. The passionate person is one who tends to be rash, haughty, domineering and ambitious. The apathetic tends to be cold and calculating, obstinate and spiteful. The choleric is rather extraverted, kind, moody and somewhat unstable. The sanguine has tendencies to being hopeful, optimistic, striving and energetic. The sentimental leans toward impulsivity, sensitivity, depression and pessimism. The phlegmatic tends to be stolid, constant, faithful and reliable. The nervous type tends toward being impulsive, idealistic, sporadic, immature and impressionistic. Of the eight types, the one most frequently found among well-adjusted seminarians is the phlegmatic; next in order comes the sanguine. The author keeps insisting that by proper study and direction, the person may radically change his basic personality type, and this has been demonstrated many times over in seminaries and elsewhere throughout the world.

In chapter III there is a more penetrating analysis of deviating traits, found in certain persons, and a standardized test for evaluating such deviations is discussed rather thoroughly. In chapter IV there is a battery of nine tests, some paper and pencil and some requiring instrumental facilities. This battery has actually been used rather widely in research at Loyola, and one of these research projects, involving some 50 seminarians and the same number of college students, is described rather fully. Chapter V contains tables and figures, and chapter VI gives samples of some tests described in the book.

The conclusion of this preface brings its author to a very practical question. It is that of finding out, with the aid of science and educational research, what will be the best manner in which directors of seminaries and their administrators, can deal with the question of suitable selection and guidance of seminarians. Certainly this little volume does not give all the answers. It does, however, supply a groundwork for the continuing study of the way in which the Church can best prepare her ministers for the arduous work to which they have to dedicate themselves in this rapidly changing world. And we mean that the priesthood does really require a deep-seated dedication of the whole person, today more than ever before; this is by reason of the fact that social and economic pressures are being brought to bear upon the clergy today, in a manner that probably could not have been foreseen a decade ago. And the Church must equip herself with the best possible means of coping with the new problems which come up; some of them stem from sudden radical changes in the world today, but others arise simply because of the nature of man, his psychological and psycho-physical make-up or constitution. It is not to be expected that the Roman Catholic Church can remain indifferent to the newer findings of science, those resulting from psychology and medicine, as well as from other kinds of scientific research. These are affecting the behavior of human beings in ways that most of us would never have suspected a decade ago.

† Ernest J. Primeau
Bishop of Manchester

ACKNOWLEDGEMENTS

The author is indebted to the Director of Loyola University Press, for permission to reprint Figures 1 and 2. He also wishes to express his sincerest gratitude to the following: The students who participated in the experiment; Mr. Martin Doherty for proofreading and preparing the index; to Miss MaryBeth Paul who arranged the statistical material for data processing; to Mrs. Casimir Kotowski who typed the manuscript; to all the psychology department's graduate assistants, who labored in preparing the original manuscript and drawing the graphs and setting up the experiments. The help rendered by the professors who gave of their time for the group testing was invaluable; finally Professor Frank J. Kobler, director of the clinical training program at Loyola, deserves the highest possible praise. It was he who laboriously went over the collected data and helped in the interpretation of the results. Without his assistance the book could not have been written.

It goes without saying that the facilities for testing and performing the physiological part of the experiments were supplied generously by the Department of Loyola University; some of them were partly paid for by the National Institute of Mental Health grant mentioned in the first page of the text.

V. V. Herr, S.J., Ph.D.
Loyola University

CONTENTS

Foreword / v

Preface / xi

Acknowledgements / xv

Chapter I General Notions of the Normal / 1

Chapter II Personality, Character and Temperament Types / 31

Chapter III Trait Complexes that are not Well Stuited to Religion / 63

Chapter IV A Battery of Validated Tests in Use at Loyola / 87

Appendices with Sample Tests / 119

Glossary / 145

Bibliography / 151

Index / 155

CHAPTER I

GENERAL NOTION OF THE NORMAL

BASIC NOTIONS

Personality is an abstract term meaning a quality of a being designated as a person. Similarly, circularity is a quality of an object designated as a circle, and vitality a quality of a being that is alive or has life. Keeping away from all historical and philosophical disputes, we shall be able to say those *nouns* ending in -ty and/or -ness signify abstractness as opposed to concreteness.

To push the thought a bit further, one might assert that humanity (or humanness) signifies a quality shared in common by *all* human beings, whereas individuality, when applied to humans, or individualness, designates quite the opposite, namely *that* quality or attribute whereby a being is unique, singular. He has a nature in common with any other human being, but he is an individual.

Keeping our minds firmly anchored in this basic distinction while using language — and perhaps in *any* so-called *verbal* form of communication — we now see that *nouns* can be either abstract or concrete, depending upon the intention of the communicator. Similarly, either the one *or the other* may be capable of referring to a singular (individual) or to the plural (universal, all, any).

Now having cleared away some, at least, of the umbrage

surrounding much of philosophical and theological speculation on personality, without bothering to discuss the deeper and more complex relationship between the notions of concrete substance and abstract nature, concrete and abstract qualities, or between unity and multiplicity, we may sketch at least a few of the more readily acceptable notions of personality.

It would be fairly accurate to say at the outset that practical (or applied) psychologists will speak most often in terms of the observable (quantifiable) attributes of the concrete (individual or generalized) personality, more properly called the PERSON. Whereas, the philosopher and theologian will speak more often in terms of the inner core, the universalized inferred abstract quality called PERSONALITY. Both will at times allow themselves the privilege of speculating about the UNITY (organization factor), or the UNIQUENESS (incommunicable factor) or the STRATIFICATION (horizontal and permanent levels of being) and of DEVELOPMENT (the dynamic functional transitional factor).

It will also be very appropriate here to give a common sense distinction between the three concepts of personality, character and temperament, as these terms will be used in the present discussion. Even though the three concepts are capable of being clearly distinguished in the ideal or conceptual sphere of human thinking, they are all really (in concrete existing persons) so intermingled that they defy analysis into separate factors. Nevertheless, should the reader fail to distinguish them in his thinking and speaking about *persons* in general, he would be likely to give the impression that he did not differentiate various aspects of reality, or at least tended to confuse certain psychological concepts. It is well know that European writers tend to identify the three concepts. This may be due to the tendency quite prevalent on the continent, to favor a "Holistic or Gestalt" view of man. Some sad consequences of this tendency are found in the theories of a few notable writers, who stress the notion of value in discussing human behavior. The reason why the consequences of such a position are not good, is that every action of the person, being equally grounded in the totality of the personality, will be either good or bad. Thus emotional traits, such as anger, or egocentrisms like selfishness, would have to be considered on a par with other valued actions; there would be no reason for distinguishing a neutral from a moral act. W. Stern is such a Gestaltist who holds that there are layers of personality, from lowest sensory to highest rational, but that they are all so intermingled with each other that there is left no solid grounds for an ethic. If a person's character is noble and inspiring, truly helpful to society, so would be his emotions also, his selfishness and anger.

Briefly, temperament refers to the emotional aspects of the human being, as they have been developed through the complex interaction of genetic, maturational and learning factors. Character refers to those qualities, whether emotional or not, that have been developed, matured, or learned under the guiding influence of reason, or thought, or simply "principles," whether these be right or wrong. But personality refers to the totality of all that is here and now capable of being observed, and described by whatever technique or test that can be devised and used. Personality profiles, charts of traits, graphs and the like are some of these methods and they will be described in the following pages. It must also be remembered that they have no more validity, in the long run, than statements made by the person who took the test. More of this later.

PRECISE MEANING OF MENTAL HEALTH

In discussing the meaning of mental health, as opposed to mental illness, much heated argument has occurred. This seems rather to be related to the general debate medical men have carried on down the ages regarding the precise nature of disease. Historically, it has been thought to be anything from an obsession or possession by a demon, to a germ or bacterially initiated decay process. Much of this debate might well have been avoided, had the persons concerned agreed on the fundamental concepts of the nature of life.

For the present writer, life means organization from within, of variously complex and self-sustaining processes. It involves of necessity a continuously self-perfecting activity, in order that the living being may be able to restore itself when its existence is threatened from outside, as well as to repair itself when subjected to the ordinary and extraordinary stress of daily living.

With this essentially vitalistic concept of life in mind we have described health in general, as the state in which a living organism is functioning properly at all levels of its existence. It has the various systems and part processes harmoniously geared toward each other, so that it can sustain itself in its normal environment, exercise its functions of growing and maturing; in a word, living beings serve one another by their contributions, and man who himself shares life with all of them, makes use of them in whatever way he chooses, in order to further his own ends. Man alone is master of his environment, both the living and non-living elements thereof.

With this non-mechanistic concept of life in mind, it will not be too difficult to get a clear notion of what health means. It signifies the proper functioning of all the organs and organ systems, so that they enable the individual to sustain itself for a time, and to make some contribution to the larger sphere in which it exists. Illness is nothing more than the failure of one or other part, to contribute its share to the whole self-sustaining process, or even it may mean that one part-process is actually hindering the carrying out of another; one single inner action, or only a few, are blocking another or several others. If disease is not removed, death may result prematurely. The gradual slowly progressing inner changes that lead inevitably to general deterioration, are labelled aging rather than illness. In a word, from the moment of birth onward, the living organism is slowly but surely dying. As biologists have been wont to say from time immemorial, when dissimilative processes get predominace over assimilative ones, the organism approaches death. When the latter predominates, he is maturing. During a large part of the organism's existence it is in a kind of balance (homeostatic condition) as regards all its complex processes, it is a healthy adult.

All this round about way of speaking merely amounts to the following: healthy organisms live in a condition in which all the complicated organ systems function in the way in which they are expected to function, for the well-being of the whole. Digestive organs prepare the food for assimilation, excretory organs remove accumulated waste materials, the circulatory system transmits food to all organs and also removes the waste materials.

Why this long discourse on health? Simply because the meaning of illness cannot be made clear without it. Much less can the meaning of *mental* health and illness.

One may go on now to state with precision and clarity that mental health means that those activities and habit systems called mental are functioning in the manner that is expected, for those species of life which have minds. They not only achieve their individual goals, the sense power responds to its proper stimulus, etc.; they also contribute to the well-being of the whole — the sentient organism experiences sensation. If the organism belongs to a species that is expected to act rationally, it does so. Its rational powers are, moreover, integrated with the others. It performs as a whole efficiently, and without lapsing for long into the state from which *no* rational action can be evoked. It acts now with full awareness (mental life) and again, without this quality. When healthy it can always be aroused to this level; when ill, it lacks arousability; (when dead, or in deep coma, it lacks it terminally).

To summarize, the mentally healthy person functions in an efficient manner, utilizing all his functions in a way that contributes to the good of the whole. In complex society, he functions, when up to the social norms, in a way that benefits the group also. Man being by nature social this is the least that can be expected.

The mentally ill person is, first of all, unable to do these things; but in addition he actually harms, or even does permanent harm, to the group in which he lives, and also at times to his own very self. Not only do his powers fail to function as expected, they develop trends (symptoms) which make it impossible even to live with others, or with oneself. This is the briefest way in which all kinds of mental illness can be described. Let the reader compare this description with that of the authorities in the mental health sciences. The ones referred to are the experts chosen to survey the overall mental health of five of the largest states in the union. They agree with the present writer in stressing the efficiency element of mental health, but they follow the traditional medical view regarding illness, namely to categorize the symptoms. For one reading between the lines, however, it is easy to see how each one of these categories of symptoms points to one or other kind of loss of functions expected. The paranoid is unduly suspicious, the schizoid is confused emotionally. The paretic lacks brain function, the neurotic is unduly anxious and sensitive, etc., etc. One of the main findings of a national health research organization in these five states was that the medical profession of the present date is totally inadequate to cope with the vast increment in mental illness, and that ancillary disciplines such as clergy and educators generally, must share the burden and come to the rescue. As a matter of fact, at the present time, the investigators assert, educators and psychologists are doing the vast majority of that thing which the community in general would likely call preventive mental health training. Subsequent action following upon this national survey has resulted in the establishment of numerous out-patient mental health centers, as well as a special commission[1] in the American Medical Association called that on religion and mental health, and another on religion and psychiatry.

It is to be expected that in the future, more collaboration between all these professions will be forthcoming. Clergymen have for a long time been trying to train their seminarians better, in the rules and principles of mental health. Only very recently have members of the medical professions asked for and received some special training in the relationship between religion and

---

1. Ewalt, J. R. (Ed.) Director, Joint Commission on Mental Illness and Health, **Second Annual Report of the Commission,** Dec. 1957. Published by the Commission Headquarters, 808 Memorial Drive, Cambridge 39, Mass.

mental health. This improved liaison can only lead to more efficient treatment of the general public, by members of both professions.

Some probable basis for the former lack of collaboration was the clergyman's doubts about the psychiatrists' point of view concerning morality. For example, if a certain action of man would be called wicked by the one, it might be deemed only a symptom by the other. It is agreed today that the clergyman's function of making moral judgments does not preclude the kind of treatment of illness which is really best for the patient. Actually, however, most clergymen look upon morality as something having divine sanctions, whereas psychiatrists often approach the problem without need for divine authority and this may be a cause of poor communication between the two professions.

Another cause of friction has been the attitude of psychiatrists toward sex. What this means for him may be seen from the following: "Sex is... Premiums of pleasure, over and above its sheer usefulness, that a person may derive from any behavior. He does not see sexuality as confined to sex in the genital sense, but thinks of the latter as a particular expression of a general pleasure-seeking urge, which, even as early as the first year, begins to be expressed, primitively to be sure, in terms of gratification with another person."[2]

Some conflicts also arise between the two professions as a result of the attitude each takes with respect to aggression or hostility in contrast with sexuality; they are to each other as hate is to love or *caritas*, according to psychiatry. When deviations of either occur, long and costly treatment is required. Thus, patients sometimes appeal to the clergyman for help. He will be of very little assistance, and may even do harm, especially in cases in which the patient's behavior takes a turn that is at odds with good or useful standards. If the illness does not involve

---

2. **Psychiatry and Religion,** by Committee on psychiatry and religion, Group for the Advancement of Psychiatry, Public Office, 104 E. 25th Street, New York, N.Y. page 345.

the character of the sick person, there may be little difficulty in the collaboration. Whereas if it does, there may arise debates and arguments between the two professionals. For instance, a clergyman may deal with a certain bit of behavior as if it involved a moral problem, and the psychiatrist, seeing it as a symptom, may prescribe from his own experience and knowledge of science. The present writer has dealt with many psychiatrists over a period of 30 years, and is glad to admit that no such conflicts occurred. He himself looks upon the study of the relation between religion and mental health as one in which valuable research needs to be done, and is being done at the present time. Religion is a source of research data that needs to be handled, not in the cold indifferent manner of modern science, but by one who realizes the role which values play in the lives and health of all of us.

THE MARKS OF MENTAL HEALTH

We may not pass lightly over the question so personally pertinent to each one of us, namely what signs can one use to discover to what degree he himself may be mentally healthy or the opposite? In the light of the previous discussions, this may seem an absurd question. However, if we take a stand on the meaning of the terms, and trust the reflective power of human beings, to communicate to others what really goes on in their minds, then some useful guides can be given at least. We refer here to the numerous paper-and-pencil tests of personality, such as the ones used in our present study of seminarians. In our present study we were mostly concerned with those traits of man which have a special bearing upon his ability to persevere in the religious or priestly vocation. Other inventories are available which enable the interpreter to put the person on a scale of adjustment, from low to high, if he answers certain questions positively or negatively. Some instances of such questions might be: Do you have tunes running through your mind, and find it hard to get rid of them? Or: Do you find it hard to stop a certain task once you have gotten it well under way? Or: Do you have a certain dream recurring persistently year after year?

One of the widely used personality inventories such as the California tries to estimate total adjustment in two areas. Each area contains several facets and each facet uses a few questions validated by experts, as to meaning and by trial runs on subjects upon whom it was to be used. The items are grouped under two broad headings, and these are personal adjustment, and social adjustment. By analyzing the personal items, and the social items, one is able to grasp what the authors mean by personality in some such personality tests. The personality traits are numbered consecutively:

I. *Personality Adjustment*

1A. Self-reliance: A person endowed with this trait would show by his overt behavior that he can do things independently of others, depend upon himself in a variety of situations. He is also emotionally stable and responsible in his behavior.

1B. Sense of Personal Worth: Such a person feels that he is merely getting his due, if he is well regarded by others, when they have faith in him, if he believes himself above average in many qualities; to feel this worth-whileness makes him feel capable and reasonably attractive.

1C. Sense of Personal Freedom: With this quality a person feels fine when he is allowed to have a reasonable share in determining his own conduct and in setting the general policies that shall govern his whole life. Such freedom includes the right to choose his own friends and to have at least some spending money.

1D. Feeling of Belonging: In enjoying the love of his family, such a one feels that he belongs; he usually gets along well with teachers and employers, feels proud of his school or place of business. He also has a cordial relationship with people in general, especially his friends and well-wishers.

1E. Freedom from Withdrawing Tendencies: A person who

tends to withdraw is said to substitute the joys of a fantasy world for actual successes in real life. He is usually sensitive and lonely and overly much given to self-concern.

1F. Freedom from Nervous Tendencies: A person with these tendencies suffers from one or more physical symptoms, such as loss of appetite, frequent eye strains, chronic fatigue and inability to sleep. He may actually be exhibiting physical symptoms of deep emotional conflicts of long standing.

II. *Social Adjustment*

2A. Social Standards Adequate: Such persons understand and appreciate the rights of others and see the necessity at times of subordinating certain desires and needs to those of the group. They clearly distinguish right and wrong.

2B. Social Skills Adequate: This quality shows itself when the person shows a liking for people, puts himself out to assist them, when he is diplomatic in dealing with friends, as well as strangers. He, too, subordinates egotistic tendencies in favor of group activities.

2C. Freedom from Anti-social Tendencies: Such persons do not bully others, nor have frequent quarrels nor become disobedient to superiors, nor destructive of property. They feel satisfied especially when they are fair to others, and not a hindrance to them.

2D. Good Family Relations: Such persons feel secure and wanted at home, and self-respecting when they contribute to the whole family situation; parents in such homes are neither too lenient nor too strict in their control.

2E. Good School Relations: These persons feel liked at school, by teachers as well as peers, and find school work usually adapted to their own level of interest and maturity. They also feel that their own lives count for something in the life of the institution as a whole.

2F. Good Community Relations: This quality seems self-evident, taking pride in community improvements and being tolerant in dealing with outsiders, as well as respectful of laws and regulations that pertain to the common good.

Another inventory which is presently in the status of a research instrument, is that of F. C. Thorne.[3]

While the layman might find it impossible to see how such questions would have much bearing upon adjustment, the facts are against him. When adjustment is measured with behavior and achievement as the criteria, it becomes evident that this kind of questioning is relevant. But this is the story of testing personality and it is long and involved. The most we need to know now is that by means of various suggestive techniques, the personality tester actually does predict types of aberrant behavior and can steer the client (or patient) around and over most difficult obstacles to his own adjustment and contentment. In other words, counsel and guidance are available, to the person who chooses to seek and find help.

In the last analysis counselors will be likely to follow the rule that they, the counselors, only help the sufferer to help himself. Nevertheless, this indirect route to mental health, taken by those who have suffered severe emotional maladjustments, seems to be the most successful one. This statement is made in view of the fact that countless other routes have been tried, such as the direct authoritarian method — telling the patient, day by day, what to do and what to say — and purely medical-mechanical modes of treatment, sedation and stimulation. It would not contribute much to this study to enter this wide field of psychotherapy. Again the positive method is stressed, that is, habits and patterns of behavior and thought, which enable each person to grow constantly in normal self-respect and fulfillment and service to humanity. By self-fulfillment is meant that which brings the human person to a state of contentment, with the past and present. In his state there is less

---

3. A sample of this inventory will be found in the Appendix, and the reader may gain some preliminary impressions of his own about social and self-regarding attributes by checking the items for himself.

harboring of resentments against anyone, and more laboring with zeal for further achievements in the service of one's fellow man. There will be hope and self-assurance, because of past successes, and also love shown through self-giving. Thus each person, with his own peculiar and unique form of adjustment, to all kinds of situations and problems, becomes an *ego* which is powerful beyond estimate, resourceful and creative, joyous and blissful almost beyond belief, ready for the call of his master at any moment and anywhere.

PRACTICAL NOTIONS OF PERSONALITY

One of the most confusing areas of modern psychology is that of personality. The popular notion runs all the way from one's popularity or social stimulus value, to one's skill and efficiency in leadership situations. And just as there are notions of leadership extending all the way from creativity in science to the ability to get things done by others, so there are notions of personality that stress originality and creativity, and again other notions that stress efficiency and skill. The man on the street probably most often looks upon the meaning of personality as something in a man that helps him to be well-liked by the majority of those who know and deal with him, and to secure cooperation of others who are widely different from himself and from one another.

In the last analysis Fr. Devlin probably has as good a definition as any. The late Dr. (Fr.) Devlin (1964) stressed the practical in all his writings. We quote him because he was fully trained in at least three disciplines, namely Psychiatry, Psychology and Social Work; and because it is a fact that he shortened his own life in his great zeal for the cause of mental health, having carried a full-time teaching load in Psychology, seeing 30 clients a week, and devoting his spare time to writing and research. Words cannot tell what kind of personality dynamics made him go at this terrific pace right up to the time of his death, quietly in bed one morning, while one of his clients was waiting for him in the parlor for a therapeutic session. And to make his demise the more regrettable, there was the prediction by his own physician, that unless he took three months vacation in order to revive his own physical powers, he would be dead in a month. What kind of motivation made him reject the warning of his own physician, when he himself would have given the same advice to himself? Only the goodness of God can fathom these forms of behavior. This is the case very often, as is well known: the doctors cannot follow their own advice.

For Fr. Devlin, personality is an individual human nature in action, with the unique dynamic organization of all its abilities and powers on the vegetative, sensory-motor and rational levels, developed mostly because of the drive for self-actuation, and revealed in observable and secret forms of behavior. Other important authors stress the uniqueness of the organization (the non-replicability); still others stress the notion of *selfness* in all the strivings of the human individual. We may be permitted to pass over these differences among authors, for the sake of simplicity and of getting across to our readers the magificent notion of "personal service." This notion is so crucial in all attempts to diagnose, ferret out, pin-point, and accurately label the characteristic quality of the clergyman. No doubt can possibly exist about the fact that a minister is first and foremost a servant, helper, supporter of man. For this was he called and ordained. Just how he goes about using his precious gift of serving, will be a matter of training and hereditary endowments, interacting with each other on both the conscious and the unconscious levels. Yet the popular image of him is of a dedicated worker for God and man.

Previously there was reference to the distinction between temperament and character, the one being mostly inherited (emotional endowment) the other being mostly acquired (thoughtful patterning of behavioral properties). This basic distinction must be kept clearly in mind as we work our way through this "workable" model of the minister's personality profile. We do not think it helpful to revert again to the distinction we have made between personality, temperament and character.

They are all so interwoven that *no* measurement technique to date can clearly separate them. What we mean is that a given person here and now, age 32, blows his stack at the thought of RACIAL MIXTURE (miscegenation) because of processes within him, which are *his* uniquely, and nobody else's ever could or will be the same except generically.

This is the place to insert the author's own views[4] with regard to personality organization and development, especially as they apply to the crucial problem of selecting (advising) youngsters to enter the ministry. We must remember that before any study of the process of selection can be made, we will have to make certain assumptions about the nature of man and the stages he goes through during growth and development. We shall state them at the beginning and not refer to them again in our use of tests.

We take it for granted that a person, from birth onward, strives to actuate his God-given potential to grow up and to acquire things. Since he is the same individual throughout this process, the effects of the experiences, from birth onward, are always his, and this simple consideration leads to the following axioms: experience (in live human beings) is somehow stored in the organism. It necessarily involves striving, whenever there is question of a sentient being such as man. The efforts lead to action, which somehow enhances the human being. In other words, man strives to acquire and to possess things; and more importantly, to maintain them. This striving toward permanent possession of objects, and especially of KNOWLEDGE, that is, of the means of livelihood generally, results in his actualization of each and every one of his powers. Hence the struggle for existence becomes, for humans, a value they cannot escape. To live is to work toward a goal. This goal is twofold, namely *survival* and *enhancement* of self as well as of other people (things) upon whom we depend. This enhancement, in the case of human animals, will necessarily involve the fulfillment or actu-

---

4. They may also be found in his "Religious Psychology," Alba House, N.Y., 1964.

alization of our highest powers, namely those of rational thought and decision. This is particularly true in the cases — indeed how many — in which man experiences conflict! He often wants contradictory things at the same time, such as health and injurious foods-drinks; or sex pleasure and no offspring, etc.

In summary, during all our living moments we strive to actualize all our potential; and whenever we feel inclined toward some desired object we experience urges; and when urges are ordered or organized we become integrated as a total personality. The basic force moving human beings toward healthy and happy integration is "will." The *native* orientation of this power is toward self-perfection. But all of this occurs in a particular environment and under stress, which results in tensions and even threats to one's existence. The resultant being which survives is a total, somehow organized human person with vegetative, sentient and rational powers. The central factor in the development of these powers has always been the WILL, that is the power of self-determination. Not every old act or power of the man contributes to his *personal* self-actualization in the same way as his will, his God-given powers of self-determination. Hence we shall sketch in subsequent pages the kinds of traits of human beings which flow from habits of will mainly — that is, those which were deliberately cultivated, whether by parents and educators generally, or by that mystical entity known as society. Only of secondary importance will be the qualities of the human person known as intelligence, learning, aptitudes and skills.

As a kind of model for our sketch it will be well to choose certain specifically human clusters of traits or behavior specimens, about which *most* modern writers seem to concern themselves. The orienting concept for our classification will be that of *value*. The fact that man's self-directing power always and inevitably results in this or that particular kind of internal organization of the total man, will highlight the importance of religious experience. The fact that man's ultimate destiny is not of this world, makes it essential for us to consider him *both* in the light of time and of eternity.

In our later discussion of the personality profiles of collegians and seminarians we shall mention a number of measures or tests, some penetrating the deep unconscious levels of the person (vegetative processes), some dealing with more conscious and deliberate habit formations, and still others which are borderline, such as fears and anxieties.

It will be useful at this point to give a rough sketch of all the possible dimensions of the person, which will have been active all during the person's life right up to the time of the test. We shall call them facets or traits, or simply qualities. We cannot stress too much the fact that *all* of them are in a state of flux all the time. In other words, the person is developing every moment of the time. Some of his qualities reach their peak of development earlier, some later. Thus it is axiomatic to say that he is *never* altogether mature at any one point of time. For example, visual acuity is best around age 35, muscular agility at age 25, circulatory and vascular efficiency at 45 and neural functions of higher centers probably after 60.

With these reservations we shall begin to label some areas in which every human being has developed — at whatever age one chooses to consider him. A simple clarification might be kept in mind following the threefold division which already was mentioned, always remembering the fact that at *any* moment of time *all* the processes are changing and interacting.

It was stated that the temperament was predominantly physical, bodily, emotional and largely hereditary. Under this heading one might include motor co-ordination, sensory skills and acuity, physical prowess and efficiency generally. Though one's inheritance gives the start, and places real limitations on all these traits of the human animal, practice and learning play a very significant role. With this statement we shall have to qualify every one of the other statements made about human persons, hence we shall not repeat it.

In discussing character it was stressed that each man's life followed certain guide-lines, rules of action, principles. Thus again, as one grows in experience he also builds up his own set of rules and regulations, such as habits of health, work and especially *social* living. We may conveniently summarize all the character dimensions as those that give each person his unique kind of adjustment, whether this be emotional, social, or rational. In this question of maturity, it was already stressed that human powers are always in a state of flux, depending upon human choices and opportunities for exercising them. Hence, in our later attempt to lump together a bundle of human traits, as found in a group of human beings called seminarians, it will be impossible to claim high precision of measurements for all of them. Obviously physical strength can *almost* perfectly be measured, (assuming adequate motivation); whereas intellectual acumen cannot be directly measured *at all* — only relative interpersonal achievement.

Since our use of the term personality covers the *totality* of all other qualities, we may be permitted to stress the most typical human quality, namely rationality, with its infinite variety of attributes. Volumes could be written on the notion of human intelligence. Too often this term is restricted to the acts of cognition — those involved in learning, knowing, thinking, with too little attention being paid to the volitional or striving and choosing functions of growing human beings. Writers artificially separate the faculties of man, rarely taking the trouble to integrate them again. Rarely do we see an intelligence tester calling our attention to motives and value judgments or both, by which men live, as well as by which they serve their fellow man.

Only brief mention will be made of intelligence in this book, and only for the sake of clarifying terms met in the literature regarding human powers. Basically, intelligence is the capacity for abstract thinking, judging, reasoning and self-reflection. It may be heavily weighted with the verbal factor, or more strictly pure, that is culture free. Such a type of intelligence is involved in symbolic relational thinking, and certain tests can be used to measure the pure or culture-free type.

Aptitude or skill is a habit or a special ability, whether innate or acquired or a combination of both. Examples might be musical, mechanical, artistic and mathematical aptitudes.

An attitude, on the other hand, is a set or frame of mind, a readiness to perform in a given situation. It is related to particular kinds of action here and now, whereas aptitude refers to specific abilities, such as the ability to perceive small differences in the pitch of tones, when a person is set or intent upon doing so.

Our recent advances in attitude studies highlight the importance for healthy personality development, of the attitudes toward oneself, one's religion, and more particularly, the attitude toward one's sex. But we shall return to this topic again when the specific test batteries will be considered.

When speaking of personality as a whole, that is, as including any and all of the habits, traits, and patterns of behavior, learned as well as innate, one predominant factor is that of integration. It is easy to see the effects of this or that kind of disintegration, but *not* so easy to see what force might be the chief integrating one. It has been stressed that healthy personalities have an interior or circumscribed force which maintains order (and happiness), gives satisfaction in self-fulfillment. The importance of the rational guiding principle of *volition* has been stressed. But to find some kind of single factor which might be called the Norm or Measure of integration (organization) is a real challenge.

Some think that to test integration is impossible. Some have tried to evade the issue by saying that there is *no* need for a unifying cause from within the organism. They then seek refuge in some mechanistic theory like the following: the functions and levels of function within the organism are maintained by pressures from the outer-environment. Living beings are made alive and kept alive by external support only. Salient factors in maintaining balance (health) are climate, foods, avoidance of injury, germs, and the like. The trouble with these theories is that *no* adequate cause is given for direction, that is, toward "survival." If organisms stay alive solely by reason of the homeostatic condition (balance) of internal and external (vivifying and deteriorating forces) then what gives them directional behavior? It is too naïve to think that this is all mechanical. Biologists know this is so, when they postulate biogen molecules and the like, in order to explain why, for instance, the head end of an embryo always takes the lead in development, and always gives suitably functional meaning to the growth of each and every part of the organism. In other words, they demand an internal organizing causal factor.

The position of the present writer is that there must be such an internal integrating force, call it what you will — elan vital, soul, biophore; but that there is no known way of measuring its effectiveness. True it is, mental health experts speak of levels of integration, such as emotional, rational, social. To the layman these levels mean little more than efficient and healthy living, avoidance of symptoms which would cripple behavior, suitable and satisfying use of all the powers, habits, and patterns of adjustive behavior and thought.

Before leaving this topic of integration it seems useful to tie the notion in with that of self-actuation. Obviously the more completely and entirely *all* human functions are integrated, the more of *self* will be involved. As was said, volition serves to guide and direct cognitions and striving toward some satisfying goals. As a person matures he develops more and more reliable and effective patterns of striving. The dominant pattern, giving purpose and meaning to all his striving, may be called his ideal.

A now famous theorist (Bronfenbrenner), makes the self-ideal concept central to his whole framework of personality development. J. Gasson (1953) rightly elaborates upon the former's theory saying that man, in going toward this ideal, somehow experiences a discrepancy between "what I am" and "what I think I am," which may be so great as to become disabling. An even greater cause for disablement would come about if there were to exist (but *not* to be fully adverted to) a discrepancy between "what I want to be" and "what I ought to be."

The Trait Model

In this treatise there will be taken a much simpler approach to the study of self-ideal, however valuable and enlightening that of Gasson (1953), Rogers (1961), Curran (1945), and others might turn out to be.

As the point of reference the model of the Christian virtues of faith, hope and charity, or any other similar model may be taken. Faith and hope will give humans the groundwork for the manifold other patterns of behavior found in a healthy well-adjusted mature character. By faith one sees beyond the visible world of senses, beyond the confines of time and space, toward the infinite beyond. In this life we see dimly, as through a veil. But some day we shall see face to face, the eternal Good. This remote but ever present vision of the divine, helps to give energy and vitality to all our strivings; *no* man, enlivened by the clear perspective of faith in God and humanity, by acceptance of truths which he cannot fully apprehend with the light of human intelligence alone, can be for long lazy and apathetic. He will have depth and clearness of vision, broadness of understanding, even for truths which are within the scope of the unaided human powers. He will actuate the knowing power to the utmost, thus bringing his own aptitudes and skills always into the service of God and humanity.

Besides energy to activate the self, faith and hope give clearer perception of goals. They help humans to remain, under most stressing circumstances, ambitious and ever-active; they aid in avoidance of haphazard go-go or chaotic struggles. They contribute to that so very desirable trait known as *stability* or *firmness*. And so one might go on indefinitely; but the chief outcome of faith and hope in the development of the whole person comes from the trait of perseverance (notice in chapter IV how significantly our seminarians differed on our tests from collegians in this regard).

The task of living and seeking ultimate truths and of accepting them demands vigor and perseverance. No lagging in our search can result in an enduring peace. No overwhelming and overweening confidence in our merely human achievements will result in lasting contentment. Hope helps destroy gloom whereas faith and hope build courage and confidence into citadels of strength.

We notice how often the mental health writers stress the need for self-confidence. Readers sometimes misjudge the writers, thinking the advice to develop self-confidence might result in pride. But no one rule for preserving mental health can be more essential, in the view of the present writer, than the rule demanding that each person gain and preserve a feeling (or attribute) of *self-worth*. Studies of adolescent neuroses in the process of being acquired, are filled with incidents that show loss of self-worth. Life has no meaning (in existentialist terms). One is in a void or vacuum. There is no need to delay longer upon the fact that a healthy dose of the virtue of hope will go a long way toward eliminating groundless fears. Courage and self-assurance are the enemies of fear. Nor do we mean cocksuredness, the enemy of peace and harmony among men. But the totally diffident and unself-assured person is truly pitiable.

People can be said to differ in a very extensive manner, both in regard to the amount of the different trait possessed, and to the time at which the particular amount was acquired and maintained. The first trait which has been called faith or vision differentiates them, since it includes a thoughtful outlook upon the total pattern of human living and behavior. The person of faith and vision is not narrow in his outlook, but he is humble in his search, yet active and diligently striving to come to some stable conclusions with respect to the "meaning" of it all. He is never absolutely certain that he has grasped the totality of the meaning of his origins and surroundings, yet he is ever pushing forward, toward the deeper and more comprehensive meanings and purposes of things. His humility is shown in the fact that he knows he can never by his own unaided power, actually reach the ultimate; yet men of faith are never for a moment dead or apathetic with regard to their own ability to solve some of the problems of life profitably for themselves. There is no giving up, when planned purposes meet with frustration. There is always energy, as a spirit of progress in all the salient directions which human striving can take. This is the trait of *far vision, understanding* or self-acceptance.

The second trait, bearing a very close relationship to faith also, is related to hope, which gives purpose or goal-direction. The highly energetic person is not just chaotic in his efforts at growth and development. The direction is given him through the activity, vaguely realized at times, of a strong and dominating purpose or goal in life. His sense of achievement, far from detracting from the spirit of humility or self-leveling, increases the drive to achieve his life's purposes, at least in part. The crucial element in this second phase of a growing faith and confidence in the meanings achieved, is the fact that there is direction and lack of chaos in his most effortful strivings, toward a normal and healthy existence and accomplishment of goals.

Given a person with much action tendency as well as directedness, one readily sees how vital it will be, that he be guided toward truths which are enduring, toward that righteousness which truly befits a human being. Thus, humanitarian motives will be the only ones that satisfy a rational human being, one who has destinies which are eternal. The really sincere person will therefore be very zealous and vigorous in his search for the true solution to the mystery of life. He will not let his energies lag, in case obstacles appear in his everlasting search for truth and righteousness. Part of the plan which nature and its author presents is the overall belief, nay even conviction, that all things are given to man for his benefit; the universe is by and large good and friendly; this is especially true of all other human beings. The firm confidence and hope that each person has, of being able to appreciate this truth, and to live it out in his own strivings for existence and status, are what give him his permanence of trust and self-assurance. He will be endowed with a sense of well-being and personal worth. These are the basics of the structure which will result in a totally healthy human being, well in mind and body. Thus, courage, which is the opposite of fear, as well as persistence, which overcomes laziness and indolence, are the accompaniments of a love of righteousness and a healthy self-respect.

Theologians define hope as the firm assurance that our efforts will have a favorable outcome, even if only in the very distant future. Thus it is not strange that psychiatrists not only stress the need for a healthy human self-respect on the part of each individual, but they sometimes also stress the benefit of fears and apprehensions, so long as they do not kill initiative. The person who knows an obstacle has to be overcome, and comes prepared to meet and overcome it, is the one who can survive in the midst of the stresses and disturbances of the modern world.

The acquistion of these two virtues, faith and hope in their proper proportions, helps to guarantee the personality traits that go with a strong ego. These virtues, it has been stressed, tend to build upon the egocentric basis, that form of self-directedness which is essential to adjustment to the social and non social environment. In stressing the importance for the self of such personality qualities, it is never meant that the person concentrates, when he tries to develop them, merely on the self, or the advantage to his own ego. He never forgets the position he occupies in this world of humanity, and he never deliberately excludes the other person from the benefits of his strivings, however egocentric they may seem to be. A case in point would be the auto or airplane driver who is in the close proximity of a very serious and destructive accident. He knows that he has to save himself, and thus to be responsible for the management of the controls — this he knows and feels keenly with all the stamina of his being. But it never for a fraction of a second escapes his mind, that those other ten or twenty or fifty persons in the bus or plane are part of him now. His well-being is theirs also. He could not have it otherwise even if he chose. Why should he choose to hurt any of them? Only a depraved and amoral character would even ponder such a possibility in such a plight. And no agency or firm, that was directed by responsible persons, would employ such a damaging person; nor would decent persons choose to ride with one who was known to be so anti-social and unmoral, not to say anti-moral in his outlook on humanity. The author can personally verify these statements from experience with pilots.

Thus one sees that the first two virtues, make for the perfection of the self, without excluding that of the other. This point is of great importance for a consideration of what is to follow. It must never be forgotten that even if one goes on to stress the need for *agape,* or sharing, or charity for all, one can never for a moment intend to do this, to the exclusion of the healthy and well-directed intention, to help and save oneself also. For of what benefit to the other is a mentally ill person, that appears so unstable and undependable that he cannot guide his own destinies in any meaningful and predictable way?

Another model for the ideal type of character will take the shape of a dialogue on *caritas, agape* or love. Just as the considerations on faith and hope were concerned mostly with the person's self-perfecting deeds and strivings, the treatment of charity highlights the person's doings and concern with and for others. Neither self-concern alone nor concern for others exhausts the capacity for self-actuation and fulfillment. This cannot be too much emphasized today, when extremists on both sides of the fence can be found. Some will say a given form of behavior is desirable to cultivate, so long as it does no harm to the other, altogether forgetting it may do irreparable damage to the self. Others more egotistically inclined, may hold that so long as the behavior does not injure the self it is approved and desirable. The *total* life span of a human being is one of dependence upon others, more or less *totally* as the age levels are traversed. Thus, this or that society may try to de-emphasize this or that age level, but through it all there runs that universal need man has for his fellow man.

No one doubts man's dependence upon physical environment, but outlandish statements may be found regarding his need for one another. Thus certain authorities will say: to be happy and healthy, a man and woman must unite and beget offspring, otherwise they will be deprived of normal self-fulfillment. Others with equal self-assurance and semblance of authority would say, the contented and peaceful person will be one who leads a contemplative life in union with the divine or nirvana. Again quasi-scientific writers are existent today, who claim to have proved by means of experiment, that religion of all forms tends to impair mental health, because of its stress upon restraint, inhibition and suffering. Some other writers with equal self-assurance assert that growth into social maturity requires man to strive; conflict is the essence of living. It builds up resistance and frustration tolerance.

As is true in so many similar cases, truth is *not* in either extreme, altruism or egotism. One can hold to the truthfulness of a religious dogma which stresses striving for a reward without becoming more and more selfish. The proviso is of course, working and believing in such a way that what becomes "rewarding" for you as an individual does not become damaging to the other. Rather, in the modern socialistic outlooks on life, some workers tend to go to the opposite side and say each individual must annihilate self entirely if he would avoid the pitfalls of rugged individualism (capitalism) and exaggerated socialism (total neglect of individual rights).

The traits in our model will present a middle-of-the-road position, denying that State rights alone are supreme, and at the same time denying that individual rights are independent of social ones. It is maintained that person A strives for his own well-being in this life and in the next, but never to the expulsion of persons B, C, D, etc. The same holds for all. To this kind of self-ideal may we all strive, through the very powerful influence of religious and other forms of motivation.

There are four basic traits closely related to each other in the virtue of charity or *agape*. They may be labeled: (1) sensitivity to the needs of others (sympathy-empathy), (2) justice for all (co-operation vs. competition), (3) balance and proportion among values (hierarchy and philosophy of life), (4) ego-strength through suffering and dedication to a cause. They will all be treated *in globo* under the virtue of charity.

The virtue of charity, of love of *neighbor-as-the-self* trait will be a bit more elaborated here. The writer may be pardoned if he seems to get more emphatic and even a bit emotional at this point, because of the vast increase in the emphasis being given this topic by sociologists, politicians and religionists alike. It seems sometimes that *nothing else matters* so long as a person has love, sharing, communication and dialogue with his fellow-man. We sincerely hope that our readers will not feel that the present treatise pushes the matter to such an extreme degree. Let us adhere to some of the fundamental notions contained in the beatitudes, and then know that Christ, the great teacher of virtues and character, took a saner view of the *agape*. Besides sharing, the truly virtuous person must go apart at times, as did his master, and meditate, contemplate things out of this world, in order to keep his scale of values balanced, his mastery of guiding principles from weakening. This is no mere modern psychological theory; this is divine truth and not likely to change, no matter how much ecumenical renewal is going on around us.

Here there shall be given a sort of overview of the four aspects of this alterocentric character structure. We hear much about empathy, or the power to identify with another, and experience the same things he does. Christ speaks of the blessedness of those that mourn, and are very sensitive to the needs of others. We hear of the need for cooperation rather than competition; of equal rights for all and equal opportunities for happiness and success; we demand the elimination of prejudice. Christ speaks in still stronger terms of justice-seekers, and the need of fair play. He even goes beyond, and demands mercy, if on occasion justice would be intolerable. He would seem to imply that conflicts are inevitable, yet one must not seek deliberately to destroy, for the sake of his own gain. Cooperation often entails a certain amount of competition, but for the common, not the individual good. To be of a magnanimous disposition is different from being an agitator; the merciful and kind person administers justice itself, with love and respect for the wrong-doer. To be peace-loving and big-hearted makes for real sharing and *agape;* to give and take, in situations of stress and strain, characterizes the real lover of society; the person equipped with the acme of charity goes even farther. In the eighth beatitude, we hear of the blessedness of trials and tribulations, of voluntary pain, of afflictions and suffering, for *his* name's sake; and why are there any benefits from such frivolous nonsense? Because Christ showed the way—this is the answer that history and religion give, because it builds ego-strength, and this is the physicians' response. Let us elaborate a little more on some other virtues, all contained implicitly in the greatest of all virtues, charity.

Empathy or shared sufferings are not just pity, or being sorry that we are not like so and so. That is merely being sympathetic, in the sense of being glad we are spared such misery. Empathy implies a real getting inside of the other, and going through the same things as he or she. How can this be done? Never really, but in an allegorical or analogical sense. Close examination of one's conscience will show that there are invariably a few, maybe just one other person, with whom we have this kind of intimate relation. When it is had it is recognized. When it is not had by a person, for long periods of time, then he is truly lonely and in need of a friend. We must not seem to imply that just because a person is empathetic toward a very few of his closest ones, he will need to be at enmity with all the others. Yet the human composite seems so limited in ability to love and share, that the ordinary person can do little more than select. Perhaps the saints and mystics could make this a universal sharing, in a vicarious sense at least, and this may be the reason why they are so richly endowed in spirit and virtue. Being sensitive to the needs of others is the true charity. And it is said, in all truth and sincerity, that no doctor, priest or psychiatrist can really be of lasting help to another, unless he has this sensitivity. The Gospel taught us this also.

One ought not to see any need to dwell too long on the virtue of cooperation as exemplified in the beatitude on justice for all. Intrinsic and total human dependence, upon parents or others for one-fourth of one's life, on the average, upon the deity for the totality of each one's existence, gives the foundation for this aspect of the virtue of charity. The actual experience of human beings down the ages, whereby the truly happy person is the one who shares, gives practical applications to the law of *agape*. The fact that success even in worldly enterprises, goes hand in hand with earthly happiness and contentment, and above all with good mental health, is an extrinsic confirmation of the universal goodness of that sharing spoken of in the sixth beatitude.

The three virtues of faith, hope and charity may seem to verge on a higher degree of human perfection, that is specific to the lives of the saints only. This need not be the case, and the lover of humanity, truly desirous of safe-guarding and furthering the mental health of his brethren, may find some consoling features in them, especially in the one which stresses the need of suffering. The magnanimous person is truly big-hearted and giving of self. Mental health books elaborate upon the benefits to be derived, health-wise and otherwise, from trying to work for others; to strive for the relief of sufferings on the part of others, and to put ourselves out for the benefit of others. This is not pure habit or mimicry, or mumbo-jumbo copied from the Gospels. This is applied science; doctrine which has been tried all over the civilized world; it is another case of showing what good is in valued behavior, in the cause of the individual, as well as of larger groups of humanity all over the world. The well-wisher, and all the more so the welfare worker, benefit themselves along with others. The more deeply dedicated worker, the ardent doer of good deeds, the self-giver is the one who alone can appreciate and emotionally evaluate the truths here put down.

In conclusion, the character traits which can be studied in the Gospel of Christ, especially in the Sermon on the Mount, need to be re-evaluated by students and teachers of mental health principles. They are both seeking wildly today for some sort of system or scale of values, according to which one might ascertain whether or not a person is mentally healthy. Some of them are very easily satisfied with the so-called criterion of normalcy, that is, the ability to attain an average sort of adjustment, and life with an average amount of emotional contentment and satisfaction. Far better for humanity and for the humanistic movement in society today, to aim toward a more ideal sort of norm, the fulfillment of a person's powers, the activation of his innermost potential, of his own very self by sharing. If this is the intent of the many psychiatrists, psychologists and social workers, who speak of the benefits of "hobbies," or self-dedication to a cause and the like, in the interests of sound mental health, then we are in agreement with them. The vocation of a minister or priest in the service of the people of God can be such a dedication and even an addiction, as it were.

The orientation of this book, as has been stated before, is to make a thorough study of personality and character, from the standpoint of a natural approach to the evaluation of the total person, and especially with respect to his fitness or non-fitness for the seminary and priestly vocation. In this first section there was an emphasis upon the purely normal and natural perfection of the individual, but his personality was studied from the point of view of his normalcy. Normal persons were defined as those who had brought to fruition, the development and perfection of all their powers, up to the point that was to be expected of a person who had attained their present age. Some other criteria were placed, for speculative purposes, such as that of Gasson and Bronfenbrenner; the actuation of all the powers, the self-actuation in the last analysis. Our treatment stressed more the perfection of the natural spiritual powers of man, through the virtues of faith, hope and charity. In the first part of chapter I, faith and hope were stressed, namely virtues which pertained more to the perfection of the self, not taken as a social being. In the second part the alterocentric virtue of charity, *agape,* sharing was taken as the criterion, the virtue which made for comfortable and healthy social living. It was mentioned that all these virtues would be found hinted at in the Eight Beatitudes of the Gospel of Christ. There was no intention to borrow the ideas from the revealed word of God; rather there was an attempt to analyze the virtues from a consideration of the *total* complex of behavioral responses expected of a normal and healthy human individual (See Ligon, 1956).

CHAPTER II

PERSONALITY, CHARACTER AND TEMPERAMENT TYPES AND TRAITS, THEIR RELIGIOUS BASES

In the previous chapter there was a distinction made between temperament and character, the former being mostly innate, and the latter being the result of living according to a certain set of principles. There was also given a set of traits of character by which a healthy personality might be judged. These were divided into those with self-reference, and those that concerned rather his relation to other persons, his social self. Each one of the traits seemed to have some reference to value, taken in the broad sense. Thus, cooperation was taken to mean a trait which brought a person into regular contacts with his fellow man, related to the virtue of charity, and it was thought to be good for him to have this trait. So, too, for the self-regarding traits of self-confidence and feelings of self-worth, related to the virtues of faith and hope.

In the present chapter there will be question of traits that are not known to be the result of living according to principles. Rather they come about largely through lack of knowledge, or through very vague knowledge had by the person who is found to possess them. They form in a manner which is largely indeliberate. Such a trait would be impulsiveness; whereas the trait might be discovered when it reaches certain degrees of intensity, no one would rightly think that a person had developed the trait deliberately. It might be present due in large part to heredity. It certainly cannot be thought to have moral value for the person, even though it might prove to be desirable or not, to the compulsive person. So we have called such traits temperamental, not character traits. The whole set of the eight trait tendencies to be studied in the chapter are designated character instead of temperamental traits by European writers, for reasons which we have given earlier.

There is the whole question of "types," both of body (physical) and of mind (psychic) which is merely hinted at here, but need not delay us too much. One can enumerate and specify the import of the various traits, whether or not he follows a strict typology such as that of Kretschmer (1925), or of Sheldon (1942), or of Jung (1926). The important feature to remember is that the traits are somewhat innate and somewhat modified by daily experience. They ought more properly to be called trait-tendencies.

There are dozens of different ways of going about establishing a logical framework or model for specifying these traits. Here the simple three-dimensional scale model shall be used. One imagines three axes, each at right angles to the other with a common zero point. The axes represent three basic trait-complexes and each may vary from zero to infinity. The model is an old one used quite successfully in plotting vector forces. It was introduced into characterology by two Dutch scientists, one a medical man and one a psychologist. They are Heymans and Wiersma, and although these two workers looked upon their theories from a purely biological point of view, and considered the traits which they found to be strictly deterministic, it is not necessary to make the assumption of biological determinism, in order to verify the existence of the trait-tendency. The same thinking was carried out by the Canadian workers (Brother Leo, F.S.C., 1962) in applying the Dutch model to the study of Christian character. Father Simoneaux, O.M.I.,[1] modifies the

---

1. Spiritual Guidance and The Varieties of Character, Pageant Press, N.Y., 1956.

scheme, yet utilizes the basic concepts of a three-dimensional model. In our treatment a more modern terminology will be used, even though the basic model is the same as those used by the other authors just mentioned. Three axes with an arbitrary zero or lowest point shared in common, represent three *basic* qualities. Three basic tendencies each having two categories, when combined in all possible ways, give eight possible types. For example, a low emotivity, low activity and low perseveration person would belong to one; a low emotivity, high activity, high perseveration one would belong to another, and a high emotivity, high activity, low perseveration one, to still a third. The terms high and low merely mean above or below the means for the group that was used for the criterion.

Now it becomes of great importance to name these three basic forces in any person, from which a resultant of forces may be determined. The basic qualities are stated *a priori*, whereas the points along the three axes are established by means of suitable questions which are answered by the testee, to the best of his ability.

Now the three bases which all these researchers set down, vary somewhat from author to author. With respect to Simoneaux, the description lacks the clarity of that given by the original authors, LeSenne-Berger and Brother Leo (1962). Our description will resemble rather the Heymans and Wiersma concepts.

Basis Number One is emotivity. This means excitability and subjectivism on the part of a highly emotive person. It is opposed to real rational evaluation of stimuli and moderate reactivity to the same. It designates rather a less rational or even animalistic sort of response system. No person, obviously, is without emotion, since the appraisal of a stimulus as either desirable or undesirable, spontaneously arouses tendencies to or from the said stimulus. But the slightly emotive person seems, to an outside observer, as if he were all intellect and had no feeling tone whatever. Emotions are, of course, neither good nor bad in themselves. They are energizers, or dynamos that can be thrown in circuit with any course of action. When really extreme, they may disorganize for a time. But when the episodes are over, the individual may have received some benefit from them. When they do completely disorganize, really foolish and damaging consequences may eventuate. So in modern scientific psychology emotion is neutral, and may be either advanageous or harmful to the animal organism. There is usually some bodily basis for the emotions, yet it is very difficult to attach any one specific emotion to one specific bodily process. The autonomic nervous system has been claimed to be the general basis for the life of emotionality, along with the endocrines; yet the voluntary musculature is really the medium of expression for all the various emotions which human beings experience. When a person is no longer able to read these expressions in other persons in a conventional way, he may be actually on the way to a mental breakdown. The reason is that his misinterpretation will cause in him a bit of behavior that is maladjustive. It is significant to note also that males are consistently poorer than females at judging the true emotion from the facial expression alone. Also that all persons can judge the actual felt emotion of a subject better, if they, the observers, are allowed to see the subject's total situation. That is, if the picture shows a snake crawling over a book which a subject is reading, and to which he is responding emotionally, the viewer will almost always read the correct emotion portrayed by the subject.

Some writers claim that emotivity shows itself when there is a disproportionate importance of a certain situation, attached to it by the subject. This definition seems to limit the notion unduly, but it may be one facet of the whole state, known as one of experiencing an emotion. If this actually means nothing more than that the person over-reacts, then it comes to the same as the one given above. Being too easily moved to crying, or laughing, or anger at another person, are other signs of the quality we are describing. The opposite type of person is hard to move to any signs of feeling or emotion. Such persons seem closed off from certain environments. Not every emotional person is susceptible to the same stimuli; rather each has his own "sore-spots"; points about which he is particularly vulnerable. He is impulsive, troubled, easily intolerant, explosive. He acts from the heart more than from intellect; hence he will have a greater capacity for sympathy and pity, be more friendly than the opposite.

Emotions need to be brought under control or else they run rampant and play terrific havoc in a person's life. Remembering that every act of sensory and rational knowledge, and of sensory and rational appetite may be accompanied by an emotion, we should come to appreciate this quality the more. At the same time it emphasizes the need for adequate guidance and direction of these powerful forces called emotions. To say that a person must always react, must never lock up his feelings, is an exaggeration. If it is actually true, as some psychiatrists think, then let the reaction take a suitable yet harmless outlet. When a fit of temper makes a man thrash around wildly like a beast, let him go to the basement, suggests Fr. Devlin, away from other human beings, and give vent to his drive harmlessly by some form of physical activity.

Another distinction to keep in mind is that each person is endowed with an emotional temperament, which gives him a sort of set or preparation, for the experience of threatening or lovable objects; on the other hand, many of his daily acts flow from separate and distinct choices, to do this rather than that. Such choices, and executions of the decisions, make up the diary of his daily emotional responses. Biologists tell us that the autonomic nerves are the bases for the temperamental tendencies in man, whereas the central nervous system enables him to execute a deliberate and voluntary act, such as swearing or moving the hands, etc. Thus the basis for high emotionality is not in itself a determiner of the character and intensity of any momentary emotional response. This point is of the greatest importance especially when one seeks physiological bases for behavior and habits.

Basis Number Two is activity or drive. Human beings are capable of two kinds of activity, namely those which are secret and internal and those which are observable and measurable from the outside. Both of these are included in the notion of activity. It is also similar to that of being energetic and vivacious. The student of temperament must take into account both these sources of action-tendency; the mental or internal and the psycho-physical or external. Both may have an hereditary basis, in glands and in past patterns of behavior. Some authors speak of a disposition to action, instead of an activity drive. It must be remembered that in any case the impulse or urge to act, comes from within the person, under the stimulus of this or that environment.

For the highly active person, external objects are more likely to be mere conditions for action, whereas the real activation comes from within. This is less so for the opposite type. He would seem to prefer to be inactive, which is a state that pleases him more. He requires prodding and constant encouragement in any prolonged task. He will seek excuses for remaining idle. His lethargy can usually be detected by careful observers.

The active person is in constant need to do something which will call the attention of others to himself. He is more persevering, punctual, objective and independent than his opposites. He is usually more practical, yet somewhat disorganized, and apt to be disorderly, perhaps because of haste in seeking achievement.

Relatively inactive persons may be distinguished from their opposites quite readily in circumstances of difficulty, when obstacles are presented to them, in view of their natural tendency to go into action. The low-active person gives up very easily or seeks some evasion, whereas the high-active one seems to enjoy the challenge to his skills and abilities. Action-tendency seems to be like a drive to change things radically that surround one, and there will usually be found a high and pronounced tendency to see in the barriers only more motivating factors to continue the endeavor. The less-active type will prefer, under normal conditions, where emotional tendencies are not aroused, to live the life of a recluse, meditating on himself and deeper inner hidden meanings and realities of the universe.

In the present stage of our knowledge of human motivation, it is very valuable to know just how a given person stands with regard to internal drive and activity-tendency. There are certain drugs which can change these tendencies quite radically, and a student of personality needs to keep up to date in his reading, in order to understand more fully just how these external adjuncts to human activity will influence the character of a given person. Sometimes it would seem that prolonged treatment with certain activators will be a great hazard to the normal behavior of persons, who have not been properly prepared mentally for receiving such treatments. This is a broad area that needs exploring, and psychologists and medical men are doing so at a great pace.

This is the place to mention the physically handicapped, and to think about the kind of impact the handicap has had upon the person's innate disposition to action. The thorough student of character will wish to give this matter his serious attention, should he be called upon to counsel or advise the handicapped person.

Basis Number Three is perseveration or retentivity. This temperament quality is as old as R. Cattell (1936) and W. Stephenson (1934) but these two authors had slightly different notions concerning perseveration. The former compared the process more to mental perseveration, the latter to physical or behavioral acts. For both the notion is the same, namely that perseveration is the tendency to resist change, in a newly formed behavior pattern. A sample of the test, used largely with children by Stephenson, will make the definition clear. A child is allowed to print "s's" as rapidly as possible, in boxes prepared for them, in order that all the letters will be of the same size. Ten separate trials are allowed at one minute each. Then the child is told to write reversed s's, also for ten minutes with pauses as before. Finally the child is to write the s's one right and the next re versed, and the next right as rapidly as possible, for another ten trials. The ratio between the average number of forward s's and the alternated s's is the score for perseveration. It can readily be seen that if the child cannot easily shift from correct to backward s's he has a high score for perseveration.

Numerous other tests of mental perseveration have been used, with varying degrees of success, in studying the personality of the child. The curious thing is that the relationship between this trait and goodness of character is curvilinear. That is to say, both the high perseverants and the low, are somehow undesirable characters.[2] This being the case, many authors do not wish to make use of the test.

However, recently Weisgerber[3] has perfected and factor-analyzed a new version of the test. Learning that there were at least four types of perseveration involved, he again ceased to use the test for any kind of predictions with his sample of college students. In the last part of this treatise we shall see that regardless of the four factors, all the perseveration trait-complexes taken together do a fine job of discriminating college male student from seminarians. Weisgerber's test is of the paper-and-pencil type, involves only mental perseveration and not physical, and can be finished in about 30 minutes, and is easily scored. It will be found along with scoring instructions at the end of the book.

LeSenne calls the trait similar to this one secondarity, meaning the "retention of impression."[4] It matters little what one calls it, so long as the meaning is clear to the person interpreting the test. All the items in the test of mental perseveration have something to do with "ease or difficulty in getting rid of ideas or feelings." In some sense this trait is a habit pattern; yet measures of the same, rely on the familiar device, of trying to get rid of such a pattern; the perseveration tendency is more like a habit in reverse — the strength of the impressions which resist the formation of new and different patterns.

---

2. Cattell, 1936, p. 208.
3. 1954, p. 3; 1955, p. 341.
4. See sample in appendix.

When a person receives an impression by means of cognitive or appetitive powers or both, his first impression, received while the object is actually present, is one thing; the remnants of former activities remain, more or less hidden, lost in a matrix of unconscious processes. Hence if a person tends to guide his behavior mostly by present impressions, he is said to have primariness; if the opposite is true, if he tends to live mostly in the past, by reason of traces of past experience, he is said to have secondarity. The word *perseveration,* which is not to be identified with perseverance, seems more appropriate today. Nevertheless an element belonging to the quality of conscious perseverance in a desired action tendency certainly has something in common with this thing called perseveration tendency. The latter, as can be inferred, is more deeply seated in the character, less effective on any actual conscious level. It is built into the mechanisms of behavior, and probably a basis or prerequisite for the virtue of conscious perseverance in, let us say, the virtue of prayer and recollection.

The high perseverant is usually a quiet type, more affected by the past than by the present; his life is rigidly organized and he takes a profound interest in everything he does. Rather than blow his top, act spontaneously and according to impulse, he becomes reflective; and although he might readily forgive an injury, he does not easily forget the same. If he is high in emotivity and in activity, he is a truly dynamic person with a very deep interior and spiritual life.

Perseveration can be a sterling character trait, since high perseverators are usually men of principles. There is the danger that they may sometimes become too thoughtful and deliberate, slow and plodding, withdrawn and too unsocial. Perseveration can lead to mechanization, to too much adherence to routine and time-worn methods, to rigidity of an undesirable sort.

But the opposite trait has its difficulties also. The low perseverant is a victim of the present, the new, the strange. He is adaptable and pliable, changeable to a high degree; his reactions are forceful and dynamic but often tend to be superficial rather than deep. He will have numerous social outlets but some of them may lead him into dangerous situations and temptations. Had he been endowed with more deliberation and reflection he might have been spared these difficulties.

Now it should not be forgotten that the person taking any one of these temperament tests, will be found to score anywhere from high to low, and that the mid-point, whether it be mean, median or mode, will determine whether he is a perseverant or a non-perseverant, an active or a non-active, an emotive or a non-emotive person. The earlier tests had some hundred or more items, and the scoring was far from efficient. Simoneaux's items number only thirty, ten for each of the basic tendencies, and each question may be checked as very true of the person, less true, and so on, down to zero. Thus the scoring system is somewhat standardized, on a specialized group. Thirty items, admit of any score from 0 to 4 for each of them. Thus in each of the three basic categories, the top score is 40 and the bottom zero. Means for each of the three categories are around 23. For the first time the Heymans, LaSenne-Berger and Simoneaux questionnaire have received adequate statistical handling. For the first time a real break-down can be made of the three basic tendencies, into the eight temperament classes that have been so conspicuous in the history of temperaments (characters, for Europeans[5]).

One can see, in the earlier concepts, a remnant of the ancient Greek theory, which described the four temperaments as related to the quality of the body fluids. One can thank a few physiologists for relating these same four types to the "speed of reaction" and the "duration of the nervous impulse" (Stagner, 1945) so that if one only substitutes "depth of reaction" in LaSenne-Berger's account for "reaction time" in that of the physiologists, one shall see real similarities in all of the approaches to the study of temperament, ancient and ultra-modern. The recent trend in physiological psychology, to identify neural and glandular

---

5. Kronfeld Charakterkunde, Stuttgart, 1936.

processes, as indicators and concomitants of mental acts and states, points in the direction of a return to the study of basic temperament types.

There will now be given the revised account of the eight types, with slightly different names for all those, except the four classic ones of choleric, sanguine, phlegmatic and melancholic or sentimental. The eight trait complexes will be described in terms of action, in the first place, and then an attempt will be made to list a bank of at least six adjectives, that will set off each type, and be capable of being used on a check list, when the reader wishes to identify a type possessed by some of his friends. It will be desirable for both the experimenter, and a dozen or so of the friends, to fill in the check list. Then the person himself who is being evaluated must check the list. Finally a pooling of the results may take place, with a dialogue, confronting subject and experimenter with the judgments which were made.

THE THREE BASES CONTRASTED

The Nervous Type, emotive, non-active, non-perseverative:

Such persons do not find it easy to make consistent efforts toward acting morally. They are carried away by strong stimuli by reason of the fact that they are highly emotional. Their laziness and lack of drive renders them open to dangerous situations. Being low in perseveration, they are without the steadying influence of other persons more concerned with the past. Sometimes these persons are given to brooding over the past, and they nurse their feelings into a momentary excitable state, but when the episode is over, they seem to have experienced no permanent change.

Such persons show dichotomies and even antipathies in their lives; from day to day they fluctuate or vacillate, without plan or order, so that those who observe their behavior, disagree very violently in their judgments about them. They are usually superficial in their outlook, and easily distracted from a task. They are absolute in their opinions, yet susceptible to change at a moment's notice. They show the most promise in the fields of art and social leadership. They are likely to be given to much worry about their physical health, very susceptible to heat and cold, over susceptible to the effects of drugs and narcotics — in general they might well be called health cranks. They are good talkers and good actors. They are at their best when in a group, but will display their talents only when they are in the proper mood. If not stimulated by the proper environment they can be dull and uninspiring. They are not likely to become men of science or adept at philosophical speculations; they are rather musicians and actors by choice.

Trait Complexes found in them: They are immature, impressionistic, sporadic, and they are idealistic, compulsive and irritable. (Notice these traits are not per se in any way connected with neuroticism.)

The Phlegmatic Type, non-emotive, active, perseverative:
It may be seen that this type is the direct opposite of the Nervous type, when we consider the basic temperament tendencies that are involved. And it will be best for the reader to keep these contrasting tendencies in mind, if he wishes to understand how Wiersma and his followers were able to fit their subjects into their three-dimensional space-vector models. The authors admit that these spatial areas, and the character axes enclosing them are purely relative. Yet, were it not for this setting off of one trait by its opposite, by means of questions which usually can be answered by "yes" or "no," the great depth of insight shown by the researchers on character, could not be rightly appreciated. Had Heymans and Wiersma stuck either to the yes-no type of question or to a type which admitted of high and low values, meaning a scale of possession of the trait from high to low, their studies would have been easier to interpret. Instead, some of their questions have a yes-no answer, others

have three and still others have four possible values to the answer.

The most striking aspect of this type is its coldness. He differs from the nervous by reason of the fundamental traits. He finds self-control very easy in contrast to the nervous type. Nevertheless he is not given to an over amount of altruistic behavior. This type is usually best suited to a scientific career; he is intelligent, broadminded, not easily distracted, and concentrated. He is systematic and methodical, patient and persevering: though not brilliant nor witty, he reads much, and remembers what he reads. He is more inclined to scientific than to artistic work. Being low in emotivity, he excels in activity and perseveration. He is not side-tracked or blocked by the greatest of obstacles, and his tenacity of purpose is more remarkable. Even though not highly endowed intellectually, he may become the tool of more talented persons: this is due to his love for detail and routine work, his addiction to a rule, or just simply his worshipping of "red tape" and monotonous endeavors. If the person happens to be highly developed intellectually, he will likely turn out to be a very successful leader, whether in business or scientific pursuits.

Trait Complexes Found in Them: They are cool, calculating, constant, and they are stolid, faithful and punctual. It is unfortunate that the name has persisted, from the time of Galen. To most people of the modern era, the name seems to imply a thick and dull temperament, if not a thick head besides. However, the connotations of its opposite are equally unappreciated, so both names may well be kept, in view of the two great fields of endeavor for which the types seem best fitted.

The Sentimental Type, emotive, non-active, perseverative:

Because this type's emotivity is not tempered by action, it turns toward passive feelings, such as fear, shyness, and anxiety. The person may also tend toward scrupulosity and compulsivity, solitude and withdrawal. His imagination and memory are very distorted by feeling, and if he has special abstract abilities and tendencies, they may be along philosophical and religious lines.

He tends toward sadness and melancholy, and has a natural leaning toward a gloomy view of everything, to be depressed, strained and taciturn; he is irresponsive, more than any of the other seven groups. Being highly vulnerable, emotion penetrates, and consequently he is sometimes violent and impulsive. Once he tends to retire within himself, and to daydream, then he builds up imaginary dangers; these grow and produce spiteful, suspicious and jealous feelings. Since these persons are little given to sensual pleasure, they become timid, yet maintain a very great respect for other persons. In religion they are much given to sentimentality or religiosity.

These people may be singled out even in childhood by their daydreaming, withdrawing from play with other children, love of reading, and listening to adult conversation. They may startle you with the most profound questions about a topic in which you would think only an adult could be interested. Their fickleness also appears at an early age, to set them off as inconstant and unreliable, probably through no deliberate fault of theirs. The judgment of these persons is often biased, though they will often show great interest and some aptitude in the exact sciences and mathematics. Language study is also appealing to them and, as stated above, they may go in for theoretical speculation but mostly when it can help them build up their sentiments.

Since their affective life is very deep they are very serious, are often fond of new and bold theories, either conservative or radical. Being strongly religious they are prone to analyze and criticize themselves for the slightest reasons. They prefer to live in the country rather than in a busy metropolis. They are not prompt to assume duties, nor quick to make up their minds, nor clever in practical life. Though they are upright and honest, thrifty and compassionate, they are also not averse to lending a helping hand to others when they are in need.

Trait Complexes Found in Them: Sad, pessimistic, impulsive, depressed, touchy, suspicious. One readily sees how this type is the exact opposite to the one which will follow.

The Sanguine Type, non-emotive, active, non-perseverative:
The expression of emotion must be distinguished from its essence, as has been pointed out before. It is true that the Sanguine type is usually considered to be quite expressive of emotions. But that does not mean that he experiences them deeply. In fact, it is perferred to use the word emotive, just to be on our guard against identifying it with either the process of experiencing an emotional state, or of expressing it with some part of the body. When asked what the meaning of the word sanguine might be, when applied to persons, one will usually hear the response "hopeful"; this has been verified by the present author upon questioning many classes of psychology students. The sanguine has a happy and genial character, optimistic to an extreme. This easily fades into a state of cheerfulness, accompanied by an almost euphoric overtone.

This is the place to point out that, although the sanguine person is diametrically opposite to the sentimental, he differs from the phlegmatic only in the trait of perseveration. Yet we shall see that this difference so seasons all the behavior patterns of both types that real serious and startling contrasts will appear. For one thing, the low-perseverant score renders the sanguine type a deviant person, capable of the most subtle manners of allusion, the most frivolous types of buffoonery; for his mind is quick, alert, a bit superficial, but very much capable of cracking a joke; he takes his life as it comes, will descend to puns, will always find ways of starting a game, preferably athletic. His judgment is usually practical and sound. He is probably always ready to tell a story or to make a speech. He is a born leader, if this term is taken to mean social or personal leadership, rather than scientific.

From the aforesaid it might be gathered that the sanguine is a favored person in social circles. Yet if these combinations of traits are analyzed carefully, it may be seen that he has his problems also. For instance, because of his levity and hyperactivity, he may very often have his intentions misjudged. Because of his lack of perseveration, he turns from one project to another without the least hesitation. He seems utterly frivolous and immature, but these qualities do not really fit him. His "actions" for the public and his stressing the experiences of the present (primariness rather than perseveration), will carry him a long way.

Whatever may be the actual combination made by a given person, of these various traits, the persons taken as a group may rightly be called sociable, easily adaptable to new circumstances, retentive and perseverative, prudent and wise, especially in leadership roles where quick decisions need to be made. The phlegmatic is to be preferred where long-range planning is needed and intended.

The Trait Complex Found in Them: They are spontaneous, optimistic, tenacious, ambitious, conceited, tactful, energetic. Compare these to the traits listed above for the Sentimental. They are the most extrovert and optimistic of the eight types, according to the above descriptions; also the most uninhibited.

The Choleric Type, emotive, active, non-perseverant:

This type likes the fine arts, dancing and music, presents a bright and amiable appearance, but is interiorly fickle, unstable, and permeated by the most varied feelings, and acts very much under the influence of the moment; he is warm and has a vivid imagination, speaks with ease, has charm and with social grace. He is resourceful and enterprising, and is devoted to his group, a believer in progress; one of his chief attributes is activity; prone to readily take the lead, he is also gifted with enthusiasm and a hearty disposition.

By reason of his lack of perseverant tendency, he tends to be "given to externals"; to be satisfied with inferior satisfactions, eating, sexuality, etc. Even though he yields to the appeals of the flesh, he will be the first to repent since his feelings do not run deeply. Yet he will be very kind and devoted to his friends, and throughout difficulties he will remain cheerful and gay, without harboring a grudge. His weaknesses will likely be vanity and sensuality, light-heartedness and occasional temper tantrums. If he becomes depressed, he will soon get over it.

This group uses their action tendency and persists in resistance, because they consider the danger a challenge to their ability. Due to emotion they do not weigh pros and cons, but trust to their own intuitive judgment, which at least in practical matters, is so often right. Their inclinations seem somewhat animal or primitive, in that they frequently do not grant to others the freedom which they demand for themselves. They interfere everywhere, and lord it over most everybody; yet despite their rudeness and roughness, they are generally a lovable type. This type is found to be better at following and taking orders, than at giving them. In severe cases, persons of this type are extremely unconventional, and thus would supply poor models for any regime in which they would assume a place of authority. They are directly opposed to the apathetic. They might, as has been said, actually wish to push themselves forward to a leadership position, but they are not temperamentally suited for such posts unless for brief periods.

The Trait Complex Found in Them: unstable, hyperactive, extrovert, sensuous, kind, and alternately cheerful and depressed.

The Apathetic Type, non-emotive, non-active, perseverant:

This is the one type which all of us can look forward to, with mixed feelings to say the least, for the experts declare that most older people nowadays tend to put on this character, perhaps because we are living so much longer today than we did ten years ago. People in this category have trouble making up their minds, they are given to grouchiness, stinginess and withdrawal. Their mood is more often sad than glad, yet they are not loud, obtrusive, irritable nor brazen and bold. They have few creative ideas, but adhere to them with great force. Being neither adroit nor astute, their slow-moving minds may be very distracted and narrow. Their strength is rather negative, and consists more in inertia than in a positive force. They think, feel and speak as they have always done, and may possibly give the impression of fortitude of character, when their main strength is in their passivity. Owing to their perseveration, they are less impersonal than the amorphous, and they are able to resist some of the external forces to which they are constantly being subjected; their lack of emotivity and action tendency, easily lets them fall into habits of routine and rigidity. They are pretty much faithful copies of their earlier years, and perhaps also of the whole generation in which they live.

Their free associations come very slowly, and are few in number, and rarely does one find creative images. Not infrequently do they show great prudence and right judgment, probably because these are not complicated by strong feelings. Their whole profile of traits fits such persons to the role of the follower rather than to that of leader, to hide out from the public, and to love solitude.

The Trait Complex Found in Them: stubborn, obstinate, spiteful, tranquil, gloomy, cold.

The Passionate Type, emotive, active, perseverant: (The all-positive)

This is a very rich character, and strong, which does not facilitate his relations with other people especially with subordinates; with them he is usually kind and even amiable, but one would rather say he is feared than loved by them. Since he seems to value ambitious accomplishments above all else, the danger is that he will go to excess, in his strivings. He does not often say much but when he does externalize his feelings he may blow his top, especially when someone opposes him, or does not understand him. He appears proud, tenacious of his own opinions, scathing in his criticisms; yet in speech he is brief and to the point. When in the heat of an argument he would more readily bring up unreasonable arguments than yield to evidence. For these reasons he is not too welcome in debates, in which plain facts are being discussed.

His perseveration makes him a steady worker, his activity gives him drive; he goes directly to his goals, not being sidetracked by side-issues; he wants action now, and therefore opposes resistance; yet he knows how to control and utilize his capacities.

The passions which seem to dominate him, are those of ambition; he has a taste for grandeur, and for an ideal order in which the capacities of all men may reach their fulfillment. In spite of these high goals and purposes, he is not much accessible to new ideas, because of his emotional outlook upon, and evaluation of other people. He judges too categorically, yet is an excellent observer, rather systematic and methodical, and often a good conversationalist. He loves books, will carry on learned discussions for hours upon abstract speculations, and his own introspections guide him, rather than those of the recognized great men of science who have gone before him.

Since this type has such a strong tendency to self-analysis, and introspection, he may be often gloomy, aloof, and find difficulty in adjusting to other people. He is of all the eight types, definitely the most ambitious — a climber one might say.

Trait Complexes Found in Them: rash, impatient, ambitious, domineering, haughty, resistant.

The Amorphous Type, non-emotive, non-active, non-perseverant: (The all negative)

This type is declared by most writers to be the most poorly endowed of all the eight. Much of this belief is rather a priori, by reason of the formula, rather than by reason of the study of actual persons. On this basis this type should be passive, shifty and lazy, even hard to arouse to any kind of real emotion. This person would go where he is led, become the victim of the whims and likes of his neighbors. As a matter of fact, his thoughts (interior life) are often a void, or only filled with momentary joys, and rather base satisfactions, such as gambling, drinking and other forms of debauchery. The chief goal in life for him seems to be pleasure, and that too, mostly organic. He is said to be of superior talent in music and acting, but not in composition of drama or songs. He has few creative ideas and virtually no imagination. Being of fair to good judgment, he is also fairly well balanced and adjusted, when no crises occur. Rather cheerful and happy and reserved, he is fairly objective in his conversation. He does better in the plodding type of work, where there is no need for imagination and feeling, but rather only patience and endurance. There is an element of egotism and selfishness, and yet he is not a popular or an unpopular person. He seems not to feel the need of loving and of being loved.

With these poor endowments what will one say of his deeper character and will tendencies? Though he is not so much unmoral as amoral, he is lacking in promptness; he is often guilty of neglect of assigned tasks. Yet he is very strong-headed, calm and courageous in the face of danger. As said, the lack of willpower would predispose him to the pleasures of sense, and lack of self-discipline. He shows a wide and universal sort of indifference, unwilling to volunteer for charitable works, and still not eager for honors and citations.

He usually has a special talent for sports, and spends much time at reading about them, and taking some part in them. In the same way he has some talent for music and art, but is very limited in his application of these to his own welfare, or to the benefit of society. On the whole, his native endowment would be one such that no one would envy him. Nevertheless most writers seem to say that he is gifted with a simple sort of contentment, and can be satisfied with very little in the way of this world's goods. Nor does he need to lead, in order to find his niche in the world. With adequate direction, and the cooperation of generous and devoted superiors, he will avoid many a pitfall that is awaiting the more gifted types of temperament.

The Trait Complexes are: calm, reserved, indolent, submissive, patient, passive.

Temperaments that have Affinities:
The thoughtful reader will already have hit upon the fact

that there are some pairs of temperament, which have greater similarity to each other (more positive) than others. In other words there is only one completely opposite for each type. When a type is not so completely opposite as that, it is said to have an affinity. This means that the basic tendency scores would be, two the same side of the mean and one the opposite for one type and two opposite and one the same for the other type. The only way to understand this is to illustrate by means of examples. Remember, that when the negative occurs, before one of the three basic tendencies, this means that the type has scores below the mean of normative sample. If there is no negative, then the type has scores above the mean of the normative sample. For example: Passionate with formula E A P is *opposite* to amorphous with formula nonE nonA nonP. Whereas Sentimental with formula E nonA Pers, has an affinity for choleric with formula nE A nonPers. Obviously the types, which have affinities for each other, should be expected to get along better with each other than those which are opposite. In fact it was this very feature of the study of typology, which had the greatest significance for students of social processes; it was particularly fruitful for those who do research with greatly deviating characters, very abnormal process, in their origins, and with neuroses, psychoses and character disorders.

At the end of this book there will be a copy of the test of LeSenne-Berger as modified by Herr and Rice; the test is self-scoring, but interested persons will do well to consult their adviser for the interpretation of the profile. This test indicates, at most, only possible deviations from the normal, which may be in need of special attention.

It will be noticed that throughout this chapter, the word temperament has been used consistently for the basic tendency, to emotivity, activity, and perseveration. When speaking of the type, resulting from a given person's score, the word character has been used. This usage arises from the conviction of the author, that *no* "Character" is, to a very great degree innate, in the manner in which all "Temperaments" are innate, *by definition*. It is not assumed that those scores which a given person merits on a given paper-and-pencil test, or even after a lengthy interview connected with the same, are ever indicative of either all temperament or all character. But that is simply the chance one has to take, when dealing with an adult, of even approximating anything like his basic inherited tendencies. So custom has it, that we use all these scores and profiles cautiously. Let the counsellor or adviser never, never, never take it for granted that the temperament is unchangeable, and this holds true especially if the person's particular score for one of the three basics, happens to come *close to the mean*. One or two questions answered differently could possibly throw the person into an entirely different type. In other words, a person in the type of sanguine could actually resemble very closely another in the type of sentimental. They are slightly different, let us say, only in emotivity and activity, according to the test. This warning will not be given again in the Appendix.

It is presumed that an adviser who might wish to use the tests for guidance, especially for spiritual guidance, would read up on these matters and not deliberately, at least, *misguide* any one. The person taking the test must be warned of the tentative nature of the scores on this test, as well as of the other instruments decribed in this volume. Wherever doubt exists with regard to any score then it would be well for the adviser to get in touch with the author and his staff, Loyola University Seminary Project NIMH. The writer is a firm believer in the possibility that any person may modify both his character and temperament very much, and that the motives which he has for doing so in a given direction, are the result, both of his own efforts and of his moral training. Foremost among all the systems of motivation is the self-ideal. Each rational human being has a way of wanting to amount to something, every day of his life; and running parallel with this inclination toward a goal, is the constant self-evaluation; he keeps saying to himself, implicitly "how am I doing?" When the answer is not reassuring, he is despondent; but when the opposite is the case, he glows with contentment, which in turn becomes a further motivating influence.

If readers are beginning to wonder if any special importance attaches to these three basic tendencies, or to the eight temperament types, it will be well to recall that a psychiatrist was partly responsible for designating them in the first place — if we may discount the ancients. This would hint at the possibility that the types would bear some relationship to mentally deviating types of personalities, to psychiatric syndromes. It may not be out of place, and will surely stimulate interest, to trace some similarities between the personality types and the psychiatric so-called syndromes. The reader will certainly have come across the division of psychoses into those which involve disorders of the emotions, and those which rather disturb the rationality of thought. It is not fruitful to outline the categories here, since the medical profession is in the process of introducing a completely new classification. The new points will not bring about any change in the age-old distinction between the organic disorders, where there is a definitely assignable organic basis for the disturbance, and those in which no such known organic basis exists. What will be done in this treatise is to take a quite widely known personality inventory, using psychiatric patients as normative samples. This inventory includes syndromes (symptom patterns) named after three of the main types of neuroses, namely hysteria, psychasthenia and hypochondriasis; and also three common forms of psychoses, namely schizophrenia, paranoia, and manic-depression. The purpose in bringing in these trait-complexes is to seek out certain similarities between the psychiatric syndromes and the temperament types; this does not mean that one type only will be disposed to one syndrome only. But it merely points to the fact that there may be similarities between the symptoms, those in the temperament types and those in the psychiatric syndromes. These likenesses have been noticed and pointed out from the earliest days of psychiatric research, by such well-known writers as Jaensch, Jung, Sheldon and Kretschmer.

There is not a very satisfactory agreement between the authors, especially since the terminology is being changed in many scientific circles. True it is, there is a strong bent among the medical profession, not to wish to *label* any disease entity, but merely to describe the *patterns* of behavior. This tendency is to be praised. This same tendency exists among the psychologists, but most of the other researchers in the social sciences still prefer to label certain fundamental *types* or *patterns,* of behavior, in order to be able to communicate knowledge about the development of these pattens to the educationist; it is these who are chiefly interested in the formation of the same, through childhood and adolescence. It is hoped that the sketch here proposed, of the similarities between normal patterns, and those signifying gross deviant behavior patterns, will help the student of personality to apply the concepts to the teaching of *healthy* patterns of development; this will be for the benefit of all those other professions, who contribute so much to the nation's growth in adjustment and mental health.

In order to apply what we have learned about the trait complexes and behavior tendencies of the eight types of temperament, it will be necessary to go back and examine the traits themselves, and to try to classify them according to some norm. For instance, the trait of stolidity would differ somehow from the trait of immaturity; the former would not necessarily mean an undesirable attribute, whereas to most readers, immaturity connotes something not desired in any person, for his own healthy existence, and so on for all the 48 traits. Let our readers scan, and perhaps copy out the 48, in the order in which they have been printed. Notice they are printed, six for each of the eight types, in something like a parallel order, that is, the nervous type has its traits in order, so that they appear mostly as opposites to those traits under the heading of phlegmatic, which is its direct opposite. This same order is followed, listing the traits for one type first, followed by those traits of the type which is the direct opposite. The reader's next task is to look carefully into the meaning of each trait name, to see if he could decide whether or not the trait in question is desirable, from a mental health point of view; this means the same as to have him decide whether or not the trait would indicate good adjustment, if it were to be pushed to the extreme. Let our reader go through all the 48 traits, and label them plus, if they are deemed desirable, in the sense defined above; but label them minus if they would seem to lead, in the extreme, to undesirable behavior patterns, or unhealthy ones; or in general if he himself would like to possess them or not. The effort to "evaluate," from a point of view of mental health and adjustment (not ethics or morality) the extremes of these 48 traits will be a most profitable experience, leading to a better understanding of what is to follow.

Now it may quite safely be asserted that some of the temperament types will have more plusses than others. Some will have doubtful categories, such as "stubborn" in the sense of negativism, or in the sense of persistence or perseverance; or "submissive" in the sense of obedient, or in the sense of obsequiousness. What the reader is doing is "evaluating" the qualities which he is considering, from his own point of view, with respect to their acceptability for mental health and adjustment, and perhaps just a little bit from the point of view of desirability in general, including ethical standards. Take the trait "kindness" for instance — one needs to say no more. And yet there is a predominance of plusses in some types and a predominance of minuses in others — omitting the uncertain ones. This will be enough to make the reader come to the conclusion that some "types" are more desirable than others. It will be a test of the *common* sense of the reader if he will compare his own checking of the plusses and minuses with those of an unbiased sample (randomly selected) of adult readers. Such a group has listed as positive a total of 19 traits, as negative a total of 23 traits, and as doubtful a total of 6 traits. They have not placed any of the 19 plus traits, out of the 48 traits, in the categories of passionate or sentimental; in fact the distribution of plusses and minuses is as follows: Nervous type, plus 2 and minus 4; its opposite phlegmatic, plus 5, doubtful 1. Going down the list in the order of the test, Sentimental plus 0, minus 6; its opposite, plus 4, minus 1, doubtful; Choleric plus 1, minus 4, doubtful 1; apathetic, plus 3, minus 2, doubtful, 1; Passionate, plus 0, minus 4, doubtful, 2; Amorphous, plus 4, minus 2.

There is definitely a pattern of mental health value, running through the traits, even abstracting from the possibility of a scale of moral values running through the same, in the doubtful traits especially.

Summing up, it will be noticed that of the eight temperament types, four appear to be very desirable, in relation to mental health, and four of them appear to be the opposite. It ought to be investigated further, what might be the reason for this difference. In order to do this, it is necessary to sort out those trait names, which have the most frequent designation of "minus" with regard to mental health. There will be listed the actual "minus" traits, as designated by a research group at Loyola University, Chicago. Here they are: immature*, sporadic, compulsive*, irritable*, under the category *nervous;* sad, pessimistic, impulsive*, depressed*, touchy*, suspicious* under *sentimental;* unstable, hyperactive, sensuous, moody* under the category *choleric;* rash, impatient, domineering, haughty, under the category *passionate.*

Going back to the opposites of these four types, they are: phlegmatic with zero negatives and one doubtful, namely stolid;* sanguine with one negative trait, namely conceited, and one doubtful — ambitious; apathetic with two negatives, namely spiteful and gloomy and one doubtful, namely stubborn; finally amorphous with two negatives, indolent and passive, and one doubtful, submissive.

To review, it seems obvious that four of the categories of types-traits tend to be undesirable, and four of them tend to be positive or neutral, as regards their implications for mental health and/or adjustment. One which has *no* traits certainly undesirable is phlegmatic; one with one only undesirable, sanguine; those with two each, apathetic and amorphous. Contrast these findings with the other 4 temperament types, which run as follows; nervous with 4 negatives; sentimental with all 6 negatives; choleric with 4 negatives and 1 doubtful; passionate with 4 negatives and 2 doubtfuls. Lastly, it will be noticed that 8 of the negatives in the totality of all 8 types, have the asterisk; that is to say, about half of the traits belong to a class of qualities which shall now be described, in terms of their implications for the psychiatric analysis of the traits and trait complexes.

The Types with Psychiatric Connotation

R. B. Cattell[6] had long ago prepared rating scales by which observers and consultants might rate their subjects. They were not fully standardized, but were to be put to the test by researchers. He had also prepared a questionnaire to be of possible use in the research. There has been much work done since that time, but the writer has not found any that would contradict the statements that will be made now.

1. The *nervous* type in the present study lists the traits compulsive and irritable; the scale (Cattell) for Neurasthenic Tendency, contains irritable, moody, depressed, hypersensitive; that for Anxiety Neurosis has Hypersensitive, that for Obsessional-Compulsive has fear of compulsion, and compulsions to useless acts.

2. The *sentimental* type in this study lists impulsive, depressed.

3. The *choleric* type lists hyperactive, moody.

Therefore if these terms still continue today, to carry their original connotation, then the nervous, sentimental and choleric types still may be said to bear some similarity to neurotic tendencies; and thus the person who possesses these traits to an extreme, may be said to incline, at least, toward a condition involving neuroses; perhaps a self-study, made early enough, might diminish the danger of actually contracting the mental illness known as a neurosis. (Cattell also gives apt questions which a person may ask himself in order to make a timely self-audit or self-evaluation.)

This is not all. In the traits for the sentimental type which we have listed, there occur the two traits, touchy and suspicious;

---

6. **A Guide to Mental Testing**, U. of London Press, 1936.

in the traits which Cattell lists for paranoid constitution we find, suspiciousness and distrust, leading to misinterpretation of events and intentions, and to reinterpretation of events in memory. A glance through all the 48 traits in the present study, does not reveal any other trait or trait complex, which might, by any stretch of the imagination, bring out any similarity to the tendencies listed by the above mentioned author. Again it seems quite obvious that the quality of suspiciousness, even in today's terminology, is not one that any character would gladly cultivate.

There are two traits on the other side of the list in our study. That is to say, they are found in what we have not hesitated to call the "good" temperament types, the phlegmatic, sanguine, apathetic, and amorphics. These traits are stolidity for the phlegmatics, and tenaciousness for the sanguines. If these two ideas are simply turned into that of rigidity, again one has symptoms of paranoid or schizoid temperaments. It will be noticed that here we have not considered sadness as a borderline emotion between the normal and the emotionally disturbed. It would be the fluctuations-without-cause from joy to sadness that would bring up the suspicion of manic-depressive psychotic (or neurotic) tendency.

Many years ago, Thurstone gave the public a Neurotic Inventory; also Woodworth gave them the Psychoneurotic Inventory consisting of 100 items, and someone has said that these two set the pace for the famous psychiatrically oriented tests today, such as the Minnesota Multiphasic (Dahlstrom, 1960), the Humm-Wadsworth, the Edwards Preference Schedule, the California Mental Health Analysis. It would seem that society, with all its sophistication and ultra-modernization, has not come up with any particularly new brands of mental disorders and any new avenues that lead to the same. For this reason, it might be presumed, later authors go on borrowing test-items and methods from their ancestors. For this and other reasons, our final battery of tests used to discriminate collegians from seminarians, has used three types of tests in the main, they are perseveration, anxiety, and free association; for the unconscious factors involved in the tests, the tests of the autonomic (nervous) response to the association tests will naturally be the measures of choice.

In the next part of this treatise there will be found a thorough discussion and analysis of the traits measured by the Minnesota Multiphasic Personality Test. The title of the section will be "Types not well Suited."

The Religious Implications

The conclusion will bring the reader back to the original purpose of this section, namely to see how the approach of psychology, aided by religion, may benefit the human person, in his attempt to pursue his self-study and the evaluation of his self-worth.

Spiritual writers have vied with one another, in order to discover solid and proven grounds, in the temperament types, which others have discovered for predicting success in the spiritual life of man. As yet Simoneaux[7] seems to have been the only one to have given some evidences for such success. Near the end of his very scientific treatise on the relationship between temperament types and spiritual counseling, he makes the following comment: The benefit which each seminarian thinks he has received from spiritual direction is related to the temperament types in a particular way; the emotionals among the categories, namely passionates, cholerics, and sentimentals received the greatest benefit; perseverants also received much. Those who received least, in their own estimation, were the amorphous and the sanguines, and these were both non-emotional, one active and one not, but neither were high perseverants. His samples were very adequate, between 6-&7-hundred. His techniques accurate and methodical.

Careful reading will reveal a great similarity between the findings of the present author and those of Simoneaux, especially in comparing the traits of various temperament types with

---

7. Op. cit., p. 137.

those of neurotic individuals. Just to get the students to admit that they were helped by counsellors, as Simoneaux reports, does not necessarily mean that the grounds for admitting that they received help, lay in the temperament types. It at least indicates a going together of these two variables, the self-judgment and the temperament traits, which is probably the best that can be expected in seeking relationships between the spiritual side of a man and his behavior.

In a similar way, the judgments made by the Loyola research group, as to the desirability of those 48 temperament traits described above, agree with each other, and seem to single out four of the eight of the basic types of character as being the most undesirable. One cannot overlook the important role which emotivity plays in both the Simoneaux and the Loyola study. In the latter it is clear that all the four types which had more than the average number of minuses, also possessed high emotivity. The activity and perseveration tendencies were evenly divided between the plusses and the minuses.

Not to labor a point, let it be repeated here that emotions are driving forces within a person, yet they are radically different from the basic activity drive or tendency described in the LeSenne test. In the case of the emotions, though they are neutral in themselves, they all too easily get out of hand; then they are capable of disorganizing, whereas they might also have been capable of reinforcing behavior that would probably have been most desirable and adjustive. Something similar is true of the activity and perseveration tendencies, but yet there is not the same special mechanism in the organism, for these two tendencies, as there is for emotivity; perhaps such bases and physical accompaniments may be discovered some day. But as yet nothing like the autonomic nervous system, with its sub-cortical centers, can be said to serve or to reinforce the perseverative tendency. Moreover, most of the habit patterns and learned activity behaviors, are mediated by the central nervous system, with its conscious regulative centers in the cerebral cortex. Thus there is not the immediacy, where neural patterns of emotional reaction are concerned, between the controlling centers on the one hand, and the mechanisms of action and expression on the other. What is being referred to here, is the very obvious fact of everyday experience, that emotional learning and habit formation is an altogether different kind of process than conscious learning of voluntary activities. One ought to call attention here also to the newer discoveries on the manner in which the total organization of conscious and unconscious processes may be represented in the central, and also in the autonomic nervous system, not to mention the endocrine system.

It is not without significance that spiritual writers, from time immemorial have found phlegmatic characters easy to direct, unlike their emotional counterparts, the passionates. However, the present writer cannot say, from his reading and counselling experience, that the non-emotional sanguine is any easier to direct than the emotional choleric, although both are endowed with the same activity and perseveration tendency. Many it suffice here to warn all our readers once again. Each and every person who is about to choose a vocation or a mate, needs to try to suit his own temperament to that of the other; and surely he will need to keep up the emotionally reinforced hope, with the help of God and the whole heavenly court, that a healthy and happy adjustment may be made possible. A significant factor, which will be of some assistance, unless all of our researches of the last decade are to be of no avail, is the matching of his own temperament to that of his mate (to the mind of his God?). If he be perseverant, and phlegmatic (active and non-emotive), may he persist in behavior patterns and ideas and thoughts that are hard to change, such as will not need to have any change — forever.

Science will aid in the process by just one other "reflection" based upon common but not infallible human observation. All four of the emotive types share a certain idealism, pessimism, instability, hyperactivity, sensitivity and ambitiousness; their non-emotive counterparts would be by nature, more patient, optimistic, calm, constant, tenacious and reserved. These two basic inherent forces, inherent in the temperament types, are pushing and pulling, interacting, impelling, alluring, inciting, moving and developing every man, woman and child, from birth to death, from alpha to omega, from egg to dust. Each dyne of these myriads of megamaximal forces will tend, under the action of nature and grace, to bear witness unto the divine, of the integrating action of rationality and sentient nature in man for the quest of the divine. In every human being, leaning upon and trusting the goodness of every other human being in nature, rational will and volition, under guidance of the all-good guide, which is God, and the thought of eternal destiny, will if he wishes, choose a scale or balance on which to equalize the drives to self-fulfillment, on every level of existence and action; when all these levels including the divine, are equalized and stabilized, then the whole human person may drift, as in outer space, serenely to his heavenly home, the ultimate attainment of life's present goals, and the ultimate achievement of his future destiny; to the last gaining of that endless and serene sort of existence, union with the divine and totally absorbing eternal light, peace and truth.

CHAPTER III

TRAIT COMPLEXES THAT ARE NOT WELL SUITED TO RELIGION

Preamble

In the first chapter there were given some general notions about temperament, character and personality. A division of character was given in terms of value judgments and the virtues of faith, hope and charity. Types were given, based on the quality of goodness, or desirability; one was deemed a good character insofar as he had and maintained a notion and feeling of self-worth; this feeling would be enhanced by means of an attitude of self-confidence. This attitude would be nurtured by habits of self-reflection, self-auditing, wherein a person practiced the two virtues of faith and hope. By means of faith a person comes to believe things which supersede the action of and transcend the limitation of sense knowledge. By means of hope one judges that present efforts at self-improvement and accomplishment would have a favorable outcome. He just knows he can succeed; he had done so before. And even though trials occur greater than any he has previously encountered, he just knows they will not be too much for him.

In the second great class, marked by the desirable social virtues of charity and love, a person realizes and feels deeply, that at no time in his earthly existence, is he totally independent of others. This thorough and all-permeating dependence, makes him feel, at one and the same time weak and strong. Realizing his helplessness as a single individual his social sense helps him to realize, that as a group member he is all the more strong and competent because of his membership in a group. The case is similar to that in which feeling an emotion can make one stronger, even physically, than he would otherwise be. For example, a person strives to squeeze a dynamometer as hard as he can in order to measure the physical force exerted by one hand. While running his trials, some very gratifying bit of news suddenly reaches him. All at once, without any other change in the total situation his score rises to a new peak, *never before* reached by him. In a similar way, if one merely knows that someone is supporting him, especially if he knows a whole group is behind him, this knowledge has been known to increase motivation by enormous amounts.

Hence the virtue of charity, involving interaction with other persons, makes for growth in cooperativeness, social justice, sharing and even suffering — with and for one another, toward that most desirable of human qualities possessed by us mortals in this life, peace and contentment.

In the second chapter a more penetrating analysis of temperaments was given than one usually finds in introductory American books on personality. The purpose in this lengthy treatment was to prepare the reader, both for the study of deviations from normal and healthy personality development, and to understand better why the particular tests of personality are traditionally being used in the selection of candidates for the priesthood and religious orders, both for men and women.

The time has come to pin-point the studies which extend beyond those on temperament and character, but which stress and highlight the danger signals, the early symptoms and earmarks of unhealthy personalities. *No* sane human being would wish to advise one, who is or can be known to be a poor risk of remaining healthy and of attaining success, to enter the priesthood or religious life. While it is certain that human effort, joined to the special providence of God, may intervene to upset all our predictions about human efforts, until the human being has exerted himself to the full, in trying to forestall or avoid illness and failure, one ought not invoke divine intervention.

The test to be considered now, deals with description and diagnosis of personality traits, which may lead to, or actually characterize mental illness. If the illness is incapacitating, so that the person loses his job, or may have to be hospitalized and receive specialized forms of treatment, it is called a psychosis. If the illness does neither of these things, it is called a neurosis. In other words, those persons who have such illnesses may, at times have to leave their jobs and may have to be hospitalized. Yet out-patient treatment centers are getting to be more and more the rule, for the latter category, as well as for several others which need not concern us here. There are also many cases needing and actually receiving care, from psychiatric personnel (including social workers) whom we shall mention only in passing, when the test to be described happens to point to them.

These descriptions shall be brief, but they serve as a reference or guide for the further elaborations which will be given. As has been guessed, the test is the Minnesota Multiphasic Personality Inventory. A short summary of the traits measured by this test will now be given. It has proved to be one of the most successful of all screening devices in modern times, if used by properly trained clinicians.

Summary of the MMPI Personality Traits (Syndromes)[1]

1. Hypochondriasis (HS) egocentric; sets up defenses by bodily illnesses; mood-swings predominant, mostly from one symptom to another.

2. Depression (D) worrier; no feeling of self-worth; over-sensitive to small changes around him; over-emotional.

3. Hysteria (Hy) complainer, pessimist; unduly concerned about health; tends to find physical causes for his symptoms; actually finds them (conversion Hysteria).

---

1. Cf. Dahlstrom and Welsh, 1960.

4. Psychopathic Deviate (Pd) completely asocial, emotions flat; amoral; very cold and bizarre forms of behavior; poorest control of emotions, since they cannot tolerate anxiety (*but* in the case of *teenagers* they act out; overemphasize everything, since they must release their tensions).

5. Paranoia (Pa) suspicious of all: sensitive to criticism; nurses grudges, very aggressive.

6. Psychasthenia (Pt) obsessive-compulsive: self-concern extreme, with sense of personal inadequacy; insecure with deep emotional anxiety.

7. Schizophrenia (Sc) isolation and withdrawing tendencies: feels misunderstood and fears being hurt; emotional, not having rational view of reality.

8. Hypomania (Ma) expansive, overactive, depressed and irritable: short-time enthusiast; leaves jobs unfinished.

9. Masculinity-Femininity (Mf): term speaks for itself, but this very weak syndrome is most unreliable, since its meaning is derived totally in terms of social, cultural roles of the two sexes — not the sexual!!!

A Sample Screening Project

Any one who counsels students for the priesthood nowadays will have noticed a difference between them and those he counselled years ago. The boys today seem to expect to be tested. They tell you all business firms do just this; namely, test their applicants' fitness for this or that job before employing them. The boys seem to think the employer owes it to the applicants, to tell them in advance if they are suited to their jobs. This is the time for advisers to warn the modern youth that assessing one's fitness or unfitness for a vocation is not the same as testing him for his aptitude for a job. It also essentially involves many other character traits.

Yet the applicants all seem pleased to learn that churches today and their administrators, are using every means available to modern science, in order to assess the personal qualities of the candidates. They do this in order to warn them beforehand, of the presence of certain traits or attitudes which might make them less likely to succeed in their chosen vocation.

As in business enterprises, here too in assessing fitness, it has been found that it is much more in line with the expected results of long batteries of tests, to say that they are better able to predict what jobs a person is not suited for, than to predict all the ones in which he might become successful. Moreover, as in business, even though a person has reasonable hopes that he will succeed at a certain job, he may prepare himself for it, only to find that there is no opening in that field for him. These are the normal risks human beings must take when they come into the employment field, no matter in what field of occupation.

Basic Plan of the Project

The idea held by the administrators of a large western seminary was to initiate a modern screening program, under the direction of a paid psychologist, in order not only to aid them in selecting their candidates, but also to enable them to guide their students more effectively as they went along in their studies.[2]

Consequently, they gave to all their applicants, standardized college intelligence tests (SCAT), as well as the Minnesota Multiphasic Personality Inventory. Thus we see that the intelligence score (SCAT) was considered as only one criterion, to aid in the selection process.

It has been customary to evaluate candidates on their intellectual ability for a long time already. Only recently have the other tests been added. It has become clear, that not only abstract mental ability is needed, for doing the work of the priest well. There is another ability just as important if not more so in modern life. It is the capacity to use the intellectual functions in a profitable way. It often happens that the peculiar attitude and deeper emotional patterns of a person, are as significant and effective in making the priest successful in his work as simply

---

2. Cf. Herr, et al., 1964.

"brightness." This latter, where it contributes to true insight into one's own personality, is a real aid. But it does not always so aid the person's adjustment. For this reason the heads of our collaborating seminary used both kinds of tests.

A third kind of evaluation was introduced, to act as a check or criterion, to which the other two tests might be compared. This was the faculty rating scale. Three faculty advisers, who knew the students best, rated them on a scale of one to five, with the best rating being five. They were told to use as their norm the "likelihood" that the seminarian would stay in the seminary, and become a useful and happy priest. This rating was made one year after admission to the seminary, and was carried out on the two experimental groups one year apart. One group numbered 50, the other 45; and each was treated separately and in exactly the same way. The *pooled* ratings were used in all cases in order to give each of the 95 students a single score from one to five. For example, if Judge A said 4, Judge B — 3, and Judge C — 3, the pooled score was 3.33 and so on for the total sample.

Let it be noted that the judges were instructed to make their ratings on the over-all adjustment. What they did was actually make a prediction. From these predictions a comparison could be made between the nine personality scores of those who remained at least a year, and those of their group who left during the first year. A second and completely independent study was made of the second group a year later.

The study reported two general kinds of results:

1. The difference in personality trait scores between the 40 who stayed at least a year and those who left during the first year; the same was reported for the second group a year later, this latter being slightly smaller, namely there were 7 who left and 38 who remained at least a year.

2. A complete analysis was made for the first of the two major sample groups, showing how well the *raters' pooled judgments* agreed with the personality test scores; that is, whether or not the seminarians who remained a year, 40 in number for

the first group, were understood very well by their judges, in regard to their possession of the emotional traits and habits measured by the personality test.

It should also be stated and emphasized, that the agreement *between* judges was entirely satisfactory, according to the standard statistical procedures which were used, to estimate the correlations between the ratings which were made by different raters for the same group of subjects. The Pearson r estimated from these intercorrelations was .72 between judges A and B, .69 between A and C, .84 between B and C, all significant beyond the .01 level of confidence.

RESULTS

Part 1

The Judges' Ratings and "Self" Scores on MMPI Compared

One of the most striking phenomena in the study being reported, is the relationship between the ratings and the test scores. These latter may of course well be called the self-ratings of the men, upon being asked certain questions about themselves. In the case of certain of the traits, there seems to be almost perfect agreement between the self-appraisal and the judges' prediction of success. We must assume that such judgments are implicit in the high or low ratings. Thus if the pooled rating is near the top value of 4.999 on a given person, then in regard to, let us say, the trait of suspiciousness (Pa) he should also score on the good end of the MMPI factor (Pa).

1. The case of (Pa), suspiciousness will serve to illustrate the procedure from now on.

On this trait the six best seminarians (best 10 per cent) had an average rating of 4.27, and the worst seven had 3.56; the remaining middle group averaged 4.00 and one sees that the faculty ratings agree perfectly with the MMPI scores, as far as groups are concerned. The greater the difference between the best 10 per cent on the test and the worst 10 per cent, the more reliable are the test indicators, when faculty ratings are taken as the criterion. It must again be repeated that the MMPI test scores are really *self-ratings*.

Each of the other personality traits will be treated in the same manner; that is the best 10 per cent and the worst 10 per cent of the 40 subjects will be compared to each other, in regard to their average faculty *ratings*. If there is *no* difference, or if those rated worst by the test are given higher success ratings for the priesthood, no confidence whatever can be placed in that part of the test. A difference between the upper and lower 10 per cent groups' average rating must equal or exceed .68 in order that it may be attributed to other than chance factors (at the .05 level of confidence).

It has been seen that faculty raters were able to notice and report to what degree the seminarians behaved in an unsuitable manner. It should be recalled that the trait corresponding to (Pa) was also related to the degree of emotional control and general sensitivity, as were the traits (Pd) and (Pt), previously called emotional reactivity and depth of feelings, so perhaps these traits were bases for the unsuitability rating.

2. Taking the case for (Pd), reactivity, it was found that the best 10 per cent on the MMPI test had average faculty ratings of 4.25; and the worst 10 per cent on the same, received average ratings of 3.71, with the remaining middle group averaging 3.95. These figures are almost identical with those for (Pa). Thus faculty raters were able to intuit, as it were, the relative amount of unsuitable tendencies, which seminarians attributed to themselves on the paper-and-pencil test.

3. Now going to (Pt), depth of emotionality, the best 10 per cent on the MMPI test, had a mean faculty rating of 4.39, and the worst 3.94, with the remainder getting 3.89. Here there is not such good agreement on the part of the raters.

It is possible to compare the success of the raters for the

three traits in question with one another. (Pa) or feelings of being hurt and tendency to be suspicious showed a mean difference of 4.27 — 3.56 or .71 — significant beyond the .05 level of confidence.

(Pd) or emotional reactivity showed a mean difference of 4.25-3.71 or .54, which is significant at the .06 level of confidence. (Pt) or depth of emotional sensitivity especially under stress showed a mean difference of 4.39-3.94 or .45 which is significant only at the .09 level of confidence.

The reader might have expected that seminary teachers would be able to take cognizance of the fact that their students were more or less reactive, emotionally, more or less sensitive and suspicious, but the teachers themselves were quite surprised to learn how closely their separate and secret ratings of their students agreed with the students' own self-ratings on the MMPI test.

4. Going on to the remaining trait-complexes, it will appear that for the neurotic triad, taken as a whole, that is, hysteria, depression and hypochondriasis, the best group of seminarians had average rating of 4.23; the poorest group averaged 3.71 with a difference of .52; the middle group averaged 3.96. Again it is seen that the judges rated the group nearly in the same categories as did the MMPI. What this means is, again, that the teachers of the students were able, somewhat intuitively, to spot as danger signals tendencies to depression (D) and worry about their health (Hs). Other studies have shown a similar facility on the part of raters.

One might do well to note that of the three factors which make up the neurotic triad, the judges had best agreement with the test scores on (Hs) or worrying, mainly about health, second best on (Hy), and worst on depression. However the agreement for the three combined has the same reliability as that for (Pd), emotional reactivity. These findings seem to imply that observers do notice some tendencies more than others. This point is being stressed here for the simple reason that one whole section of the screening test battery that is being proposed in this study, has to do with various kids of fears and anxieties that are found in seminarians as well as college students.

5. There are scores on the MMPI for excessive activity tendency (Ma) and freedom from withdrawing tendency (Sc). Some authors consider the (Ma) score to be a kind of self-integrational or self-organizational score. Because when a person habitually starts jobs he cannot finish, attempts more than he can accomplish, he would seem to be disorganized. It is certain that the hypomanic person—ever on the go, yet never really coming to feel the joy of accomplishing his goals, would not be too happy in the priestly vocation, unless he had some special hobbies or avocations.

The best 10 per cent of the seminary group were rated an average of 4.29, and the poorest, 4.04; and here for the first time we have little or no difference. The middle group rated the lowest by far, namely 3.83. Here the middlemost, differed in the unexpected direction. The teachers did not get to know the deeper goal-striving tendencies of their students, apparently.

With regard to (Sc), freedom from withdrawing tendencies and suspiciousness, the best 10 per cent averaged 4.18 and the worst, 4.00; the middle group averaged 3.80. The best and worst differed again by only .18, with the middle group worse than the worst group.

Just why the raters went so far astray on these two traits is not clear to the present writer. It would seem that raters could not penetrate the inner feelings and urges of their students. It will be found, in another part of this work that the trait (Sc) did actually show up as one that would discriminate the successful seminarians from the unsuccessful ones, with a high degree of efficiency, in the case of two different samples, totalling 95 persons.

6. The last trait to be considered is social introversion (Si). One would spontaneously judge that the teachers could spot this trait fairly reliably. It would seem important for them to be able to do so, since this trait plays such a large role in developing leadership ability. The trait as described by Hathaway, how-

ever, savors more of an emotional introversion — extraversion quality, than of a direct sociability quality. One would think that the quality of being turned outward more than inward toward self could be spotted. Of course ever since Guilford has given us the factors, namely introversion toward self (emotional) and introversion toward ideas (intellectual); extraversion toward persons (emotional) and extraversion toward objects (intellectual), people are very confused about this whole trait complex. Whatever may have caused the result, it has to be reported that the judges rated the best 10 per cent as having an average of 4.22 and the worst 10 per cent as averaging 4.17 and the middle most, again 3.83, which means that those scoring in the middle 80 per cent of the whole group of students, on the trait of Social Introversion, had by a difference of .34 the poorest success rating by their faculty observers. This finding has no ascertainable basis, except in the possible unreliability of the scale. It was actually one of the last to be developed by the Minnesota Workers.

Summary of Part 1: Results

The general purpose of this part has been to compare the picture that one gets of the personalities of the seminarians of the 1961 sample, gotten from teachers' ratings with that gotten by studying their MMPI test scores. In most of the traits there was very good agreement. It would seem to follow that when both external observers (teachers) and self-observers show such good agreement, the judgments would merit very close attention, on the part of heads of seminaries. We shall see later in this chapter, that the same procedure was followed a year later, with almost identical results.

Meantime superiors began acting upon judgments, which were based on tests as well as ratings, and hence the continuation of the project on an experimental basis was made impossible. After all, there is here an ethic involved, just as there would be, when physicians have proved the efficacy of a certain medicine, or method of treatment.

Part 2: Results

In this part of the study there was a slightly different approach. The mean value for each of the nine personality traits for the 40 who remained in the seminary for a year, was compared to the mean value for each of these same nine traits for the 10 who had left. The t test for significance was applied to each of these 9 pairs of means. In every case, the means for the 10 who left, hereafter to be called unsuccessful, were poorer (higher numerically) than were those for the 40 who stayed in the seminary. The largest difference appeared for (Pt), that is, obsessive-compulsiveness or depth of emotionality. This difference was significant at the .03 level of confidence. The next largest difference was for the trait (Pd), emotional reactivity, oddity or unconventionality; this was significant at the .001 level of confidence.

It seems unfortunate that the trait (Pd) has such varied and various meanings. The original meaning was psychopathic deviate. Other meanings were over-sensitivity, character disorder, singularity; odd, and even amoral behavior.

The authors are still not agreed as to the most suitable terminology. Agreed they are, that whatever name be given the trait complex, it is far and away the most undesirable of all of them. It is said to have some kind of organic basis but this is also disputed. It doesn't yield to any known forms of treatment.

Almost the same could be said about (Pt) or psychasthenia. This was at one time labelled "weak nerves" and was thought to be closely tied to organic processes of some sort.

It is tempting to review the history of the different drug treatments, that have been suggested for these two types of illnesses. Space will not permit us to elaborate; yet almost any adult reader, will possibly have learned something about such drugs, or may have tried some of them, for conditions sometimes called nervous fatigue and exhaustion. It seems high time that seminary heads begin to take it upon themselves to recognize the symptoms of such persons who would score poorly on (Pd) and on (Pt).

These findings are all the more impressive by reason of the fact that the formula for small samples had to be used. When we come to compare the 1962 group profiles, with this one for the 1961 sample, there will remain little reason for doubting the validity of this study.

The other personality variables were, as stated, all more favorable for those seminarians who stayed than they were for those who left during the first year. The magnitude of the differences decreased in the order that now follows, starting with (Pd) through (Pt), (Sc), or freedom from withdrawing tendency, (Pa) or suspiciousness, (Ma) or overactivity, (Hy) or health-crankinesss, (Hs) or anxious defensiveness, and (D) depression. The (Mf) scale was omitted for reasons given above, and the (Si) scale was added later.

It cannot be too much emphasized that the project which was begun at the seminary here described, was intended to continue year after year. Two years' results are being summarized here. The reader will gain considerable more confidence in this first result when he finishes reading what is to follow. The fact should not be passed over lightly, that the traits which showed agreement between the MMPI tests taken individually, and the mean of 3 faculty ratings were (Pd) and (Pt). These same traits are the ones which discriminated the successful from the unsuccessful seminarians. The broad meaning Hathaway assigns to these two traits should again be noted, namely, depth and amount of emotional sensitivity, oddity and compulsivity. It is now time to see how nearly these results could be duplicated in another group at the same seminary using exactly the same procedure.

Part 3: Results

The Ratings. Now the same breakdown will be made for the 1962 group of 45 seminarians, but it will be made in abbreviated form. I.Q. tests, as well as the MMPI were given to all the applicants. This time out of 45, only 7 left during one years' time. Three faculty members rated all of the 45 on the same basis as before, namely likelihood of perseverance, and on a 5 point scale. The same comparison was made between the "good" 10 per cent and the "poor" 10 per cent, on each of the traits, in terms of their average rating by the three teachers. Again it must be understood that this agreement is between the fitness of the men as rated by the teachers, and the personality and adjustment traits of the students as declared by their own checking of items on the MMPI.

The very great similarity to the previous sample cannot be ignored. Again (Pd) and (Pt), emotional sensitivity and oddity, were highly reliable, between the .01 and .05 levels of confidence. Raters could diagnose emotionality, it seems. There was also the same amount of agreement for (Sc), freedom from withdrawal tendencies, and for the neurotic triad. The only outstanding difference was for (Pa) or suspiciousness. For (Pa) in this 1962 sample the agreement between raters and MMPI was the lowest of all, save for (Ma), overactivity or manic tendency.

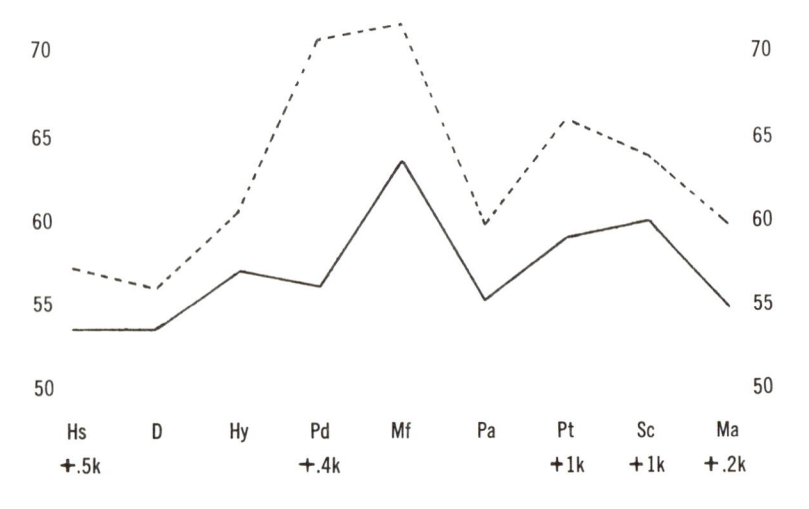

Figure 1 MMPI Profile of 40 seminarians (solid line) and 10 who left the seminary (broken line), 1961 sample

Let it be recalled that these two last trait-complexes are in the class of psychotic, that is, serious mental disturbances. Above, it was hinted that laymen in the mental health sciences, the teachers, could not be expected to have much skill in diagnosing such traits. Also there is this difference between the 1961 and 1962 samples. Each group had been given College Intelligence Tests, and on the 1961 sample two persons had scores below 100 on a relative scale, and both were rated very low on adjustment. They had both left within one year. The next year no one was accepted with a score on the SCAT below 100. Thus the seminary heads had already begun to profit from the use of the tests.

And finally, there was heightened agreement on the (Sc) scale, withdrawal tendencies, bringing it almost up to the level of the (Pd) and (Pt) scales. Thus if one were tempted to say that the judges improved in their ratings of the psychotic triad (Sc), he would likewise be required to say that they decreased in their efficiency to spot (Pa) or suspiciousness.

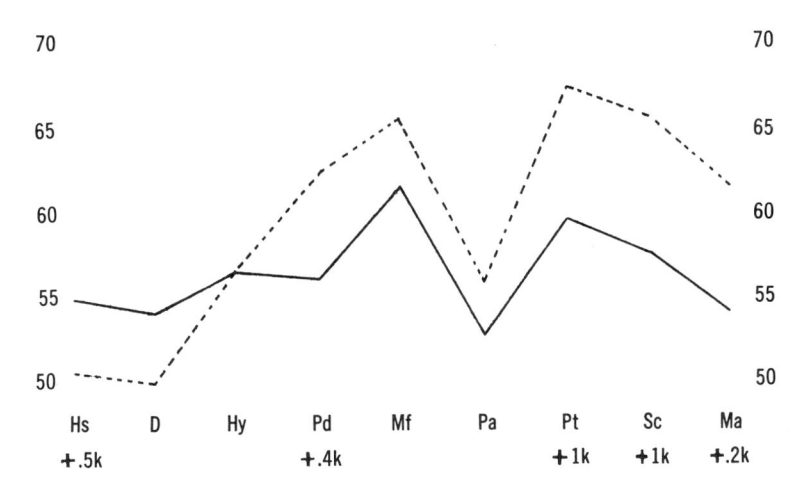

Figure 2 MMPI Profile of 45 seminarians (solid line) and 7 who left the seminary (broken line), 1962 sample

It might be stated that the raters, working under the close supervision of the project director and their local adviser, came to enjoy this delicate and nerve-racking experience of rating the deeper thoughts and motives of others. It gave them a new slant on their own personal habits of self-evaluation.

The Successful and Unsuccessful

Here we are dealing with one very small sample of 7 who left the seminary this year. Still the significance of the difference between the two groups amazes one; after listing the rank orders of means of the 7 and the 45 respectively, we may discuss the trends. Obviously some differences between 1961 and 1962 are observable but the overall similarities are almost frightening. One must not, however, fail to consider the small size of the populations.

(Pt) now turns out to have the greatest difference. The second largest was on the (Sc) — the third largest on the (Pd) and (Ma) which is nearly the same. Next came (Pa), (Hs), (D); and (Hy) with little or no difference at all.

Another difference was that with the 1962 group, on the neurotic triad, the men who left had slightly better scores than those who stayed. It will be remembered, on the 1961 group it was slightly, though not significantly in the opposite direction, to that of the 1962 group.

Final Comments

There is *no* single test which can, in the author's opinion, diagnose those deepseated personality traits which the person himself wishes to conceal. This is believed to be true, even of the so-called depth analyses, supposedly made possible by means of the projection tests. It is a tenable doctrine in psychology today that *the person himself* cannot declare the innermost aspects of his core personality traits, even when he tries. He tends to be either too hard on himself or too easy-going and superficial. Granted that there are "checks" or "corrections" of a sort that, when used by trained clinicians, could improve the score, that is, bring it more in line with reality; still extreme caution must be used in the interpretation of personality test results. The crucial problem which confronts the tester in all these projects is: what may or should be done with the results of the test?

There is obviously an ethical question here. These persons on taking a long battery of tests — or even on taking a single one, such as intelligence — are revealing their innermost selves. Not even the teacher has, according to the code of ethics of the American Psychological Association, an absolute right to use this knowledge without the person's permission. When a projective tester begins to delve more deeply into the subconscious, then the need for confidentiality becomes much greater. At the present time school authorities are being warned by federal authorities extremely often of their duty to safeguard the class records; not even to divulge their secrets to officials of the FBI.

What would be a safe rule to follow in these matters? To remember once and for all that the only person who has any direct and absolute right to know the results of personality tests is the *person* being tested, and that he alone can delegate the right to use such knowledge. Here another principle must be invoked, namely that of self protection. The testee himself may at times be denied the full knowledge of the results. This is particularly necessary in those cases in which such knowledge would certainly be misused by the subject. A common case in point would be the one in which, not understanding the meaning of the scores, he would do real damage to himself by his choice of a vocation, etc. The danger here would be similar to that in which medicines or drug containers, would either show no labels at all, or be falsely labelled as to their contents.

The main reason that our government is so cautious about protecting the class records is, of course, the fact that there have been grave abuses of data from confidential files, that should properly have been accessible only to the person himself, and to the legitimate authorities. We are here approaching the gravest of all moral problems confronting physicians and others today — who should *know* the doctor's diagnosis? We shall not delve more deeply into this ticklish dilemma, but it may help the reader to know, how one seminary in a distant part of the world handles the problem.

This particular school has a team approach toward the job of selecting candidates. On the team are: the seminary spiritual father, the rector or his representative, the student counsellor and the vocational tester (a trained clinical psychologist or psychiatrist). These four are the only ones who see all the test data, intelligence as well as personality. These four meet together before calling in the candidate. Then it is agreed that data x, y, z, etc., are the only ones to be communicated to the candidate. Only then is the latter called in and told what was agreed upon. And the candidates' permission is at once asked if any other teachers or principals may have certain information shared with them.

Readers might also be glad to know, that certain larger seminaries have carried on a full-fledged testing and selection program for a dozen or more years. One of them, upon evaluating the results found that only a little better than chance success was had. Their researchers summarized the findings in this manner. Over a period of four years, 9 very bad risks were caught and only 6 were missed. If screening is pushed too far, some very good candidates are lost. Some caution must be followed in eliminating the doubtful ones. Nevertheless the superior general of this same large order, averred that he would continue the screening procedure regardless of cost, provided that even one person a year would be spared the misery of mental breakdown (that is of the more serious sort).

TRANSITION TO THE LOYOLA TEST BATTERY IN ITS TOTALITY

The perusal of the foregoing section, with its emphasis upon the deeper and perhaps unconscious mechanisms of behavior and thought, will highlight the need to consider fears and anxieties in the evaluation of the total personality of seminarians and collegians. Next to this in importance, will be the appraisal of the total emotionality, of the person; this must include the momentary responsivity shown in transitory reactions of the moment, as well as the more permanent deeper quality of emotivity shown in temperamental dispositions or tendencies to follow inherent patterns. Finally the integrational aspects of the person will be considered, namely, his ability to subsume all the surface traits, under the dominating influence of some one central or whole-making control.

It was said that the unifying principle, the directional power within each individual, had to be both on the conscious and on the unconscious level. None of the vegetative processes of the person are directly amenable to the conscious subject, but have to be inferred from behavior and part-processes. Much of what passes under the name of sensory process is also moderated, reinforced or weakened, by that part of sensation which is physiological and glandular. Thus in vision a person needs to have the normal retinal chemistry of rhodopsin, part of the vegetative process; he needs the firing of neurons, both in the retina and the cerebral cortex; these are only some of the mediation processses; and finally he needs the coordination of the cortical patterns of firing in unison with the surrounding brain cells, and with the deeper-lying subcortical brain mechanisms, in order to make each *act* of seeing, a thing which is actually lived and capable of being revived in imagination and memory. Lastly one must not neglect the physical aspects of memory; surely there must be some sensory and bodily remnant there, in order that a person may re-live, re-vive, re-instate bits of behavior and thought, whether for the benefit or for the harm of the total organism or person.

The reader must constantly remind himself, revive the experience of, the fact that an integrated, well-organized personality will not be healthy unless all these processes are contributing day in and day out, to his total complex of experience and of behavior.

There is one last aspect of the total reactivity of the person and that is the sensory-motor aspect; the mind-action patterning of human life and behavior. The person not only knows and thinks about what he experiences, on any level of complexity, but he also acts, moves, initiates patterns of behavior on all levels of activity. It does not change the facts any, if the reader wishes to include under the one single term of behavior, every tiny bit of muscle and glandular action, including under the simple expression "behavior," even the most subtle, silent and secret thoughts and desires of the total integrated personality. There will be the "effect" of experience, based upon the residue of inheritance and maturation, and always being modified by these subtle influences, to be accounted for in trying to understand the total integrated striving person.

This small digression was placed at this point in the text in order to prepare the reader for the better understanding and appreciation of the total battery of tests to be presented in the next section of the book.

It will soon be noticed that there was available a complete battery of tests, whose purpose was to discover the latent, hidden, deeply-seated mechanisms of anxiety and insecurity, as judged by the person's own conscious responses to a lengthy questionnaire. The total field of possible anxious feelings and threats was explored, including anxiety directed outward, that directed inward toward the self, and the all inclusive total pattern. What were the differences, if any, between collegians and seminarians in this respect? Next the area of action tendency, perseveration tendency was to be tested. These inner tendencies were sometimes borderline, with respect to consciousness. The person merely was asked to describe himself, as best he might, with respect to such patterns as ideas tending to persist despite wishes to get rid of them, tunes running through the mind, and so forth. This perseverative tendency was to be explored on three levels or fields, such as the emotional level, the personal area, the rational counterpart of experience, and so forth. Suitable scales are available to help the tester interpret the responses of the subjects. It would be most valuable in appraising the future success of the collegians and seminarians, to know just how they score in their perseveration tendencies over a large range of possible action tendencies, mental, physical and psycho-physical.

Again the "quick" response, or trigger tendencies were tapped; this required the use of the "free-association" tests; in these measures of responsivity, persons were scored with regard to their kind or quality of response; what words do they come up with, when told to respond with an answer which they think most people will give, in the shortest possible time, when confronted with one single verbal symbol, such as soldier. In order to make the study more comprehensive, that is, to include the conscious as well as the border-line and unconscious reactions, physiological measures had to be made. This part of the battery, as will be seen, was found to be the most significant in distinguishing the collegians from the seminarians. It admitted of the possibility of inter-relating the scores made by the two groups of subjects, on the conscious traits with respect to one another, of the unconscious ones with respect to each other, and of the conscious with respect to the unconscious. The relative competence shown by two large groups of human subjects, when they are evaluated with respect to these three sets of scores, should get at that most necessary of all qualities of the total human personality, self-integration or self-organization, and its related counterpart, self-evaluation and successful living in a particular vocation.

Another phase of the total personality testing program, was that in which the normalcy of the candidate was to be assessed. Two distinct assessments could be made with the tests used. The one was that in which the free-association method was used, the other was that in which galvanometer readings of the unconscious responses of the nervous system were used. Obviously this latter test would have to be given in a psychological laboratory with special equipment. It was to be used as a last resort, and at the recommendation of the physician.

Thus it is seen that a very thorough-going battery is being applied in order to aid in the determination of the physical, psychological and psycho-physiological fitness of the person. Another way of saying this, is to proclaim that no possible means of assessing the fitness and desirability of the candidate is being omitted at this stage of the research program.

One more hint will be of use. At the beginning of this chapter there was given a division of criteria for aiding in assessing the personalities in the following manner. Criterion I was intellectual capacity. We recall that the teachers in the seminary were told to judge and predict the fitness of their charges, but not merely on the basis of their intellectual capacities. As we followed the description of their performance, we noticed that in the first sample, that of 1961, the intelligence test yielded a few very low capacity persons, who were, nevertheless, admitted. In the second sample, that of 1962, a higher standard was used. But in this sample too, the intellectual capacity was not the sole criterion. Several other criteria in this area were included.

The non-intellectual criteria were the following: Emotional control; (Pd, Pt, Pa). We see that the MMPI test for weeding out the unfit, makes use of this criterion, in large measure, in several of the trait complexes which it tests. The Loyola battery which we have described tests for anxiety, fear, deep emotionality, even going down to the totally unconscious physiological levels. Another non-intellectual criterion was that of the neurotic triad of the MMPI. The traits included in this triad were sensitivity to bodily injury, insecurity, fears of bodily illness, and depression and guilt feelings. While the Loyola battery does not have any direct measure of this type of neurosis, it does evaluate the deeper causes of neurotic tendency in the autonomic nervous system. The third trait complex that was described as being measured by the MMPI was the Self-integration or (Sc, Ma) pattern. This was the one which the teachers, acting as raters, did not succeed so well in predicting. Yet no one, it would seem, would doubt the necessity of having a healthy integration and self-organization present, in all those persons who take upon themselves the responsibility of being representatives of God, in guiding the destinies of human beings. Thus in the Loyola battery there is ample space given to the use of various and far-reaching measures of the Self-integration and Self-estimation and Feelings of Self-worth categories of experience. In the last chapter of this work, some easy rules of operation will be given, as to the most efficient use of these various tests and criteria for selection.

Let it be noted again, that the criteria of self-integration on the MMPI, were *not* very successfully judged or rated by the teacher-raters in the seminary studied. Nor were the raters at all successful in distinguishing those seminarians who remained at least a year in the seminary, from those who left within this year.

Criterion five was Sociability on the MMPI scale. Yet because of the large amount of uncertainty connected with the meaning of this test score, it was decided not to include this factor in the Loyola battery. However, it is well known that the perseveration test used, has a high loading with emotional as well as socially important factors. The association test also can be used to give a fairly accurate picture of the candidate's sociability tendencies.

CHAPTER IV

A BATTERY OF TESTS IN USE AT LOYOLA FOR MANY YEARS

In recent years frequent and consistent efforts have been made by most religious denominations to screen their candidates for the ministry. In order to do this more efficiently, the tools and techniques of scientific psychology and psychiatry have been used. A clear and succinct review of hundreds of such empirical studies has been published by Menges and Dittes (1965) in a volume entitled: *Psychological Studies of Clergymen.* This appears to be the first multi-faith attempt to collect information of this kind. In scanning these brief excerpts from scientific articles, the reader gains the impression that many of the studies were poorly and hastily designed, and at least some of them were hardly appropriate for the sophisticated type of screening that was expected of them. In general, most such studies have been discouragingly negative in result, in the sense that either no difference was discovered between the lay and the ministerial candidate, or that whatever techniques might be suitable for one group of religious would not be suitable for another. This would tend to make research in these areas and application of research findings very tedious and unfruitful. Since many of the studies were longitudinal, replication and follow-up studies are almost impossible. Add to this the fact that most studies of this nature, have not found their way into the standard journals, and one sees the difficulties that are encountered. Only within the last decade have some of the standard journals come forth with significant findings in this area of investigation.

A still larger attempt has been made by Meissner (1961), whose book is entitled, *An Annotated Bibliography of Psychology and Religion*. This author divides the total literature on personality under such broad headings as philosophical, historical, empirical; and gives rather lengthy resumés of the various books and journal articles, some of which are evaluative.

Again one would have to distinguish very carefully between mostly empirical and largely philosophical studies, and set up his own standards of evaluation concerning the results of each, in order to gain real profit from a perusal of this classical material on the ministry.

The present study is another attempt, on the empirical or experimental level, to delineate such subtle differences between groups of persons, as might be of some assistance in advising applicants what to do about their possible vocation in the ministry. The need for such studies cannot be stressed too much, in these days when every applicant for any kind of occupation thinks he is being slighted if he does not get a test battery of some sort. A stronger argument for careful screening, is the fact that most churches pay their clergymen next to nothing for their services, and yet long years of arduous study and preparation are needed in preparation for the ministry. The drop-out rate is very excessive, as might be expected, in these times. It is simply poor economy to accept for training those whose likelihood for success is minimal. Besides, certain would-be authorities in the medical professions have at least hinted at the possibility, that the rigorous training programs in our seminaries may have increased the rate of incidence of mental disorders in a manner that could be prevented by proper and early screening and selection of candidates. However true this latter suspicion might be, it certainly makes administrators of religious training programs examine their curricula, as well as their consciences.

The results of such self-studies have already been used by various seminaries, in order to diminish the risk, at least, of putting too much strain and stress upon the young candidates, so that they will one day succumb to mental illness.

This is the general background for the present study. The author has been engaged in a ten-year project of evaluation of the training received by Catholic seminarians. During this time, and since the completion of that study, he has collaborated with Harvard and Yeshiva Universities in sharing insights, gained by research projects similar to these at Catholic universities and seminaries affiliated with them, especially at Loyola of Chicago. He is prepared to show that some real gains have been made here in lessening both the risk of drop-outs, and of possible mental illness. One superior of a religious order, who was responsible for the final decision of accepting some 60 candidates each year for his seminary, told the writer that he would be happy, if the screening program would result in preventing or forestalling one mental breakdown per year. The actual rate of success, in terms of prediction, over a ten-year period of screening, was only one out of three mental health casualties.

The overall purpose of this study might be stated in the following simple manner. A battery of tests, suitable for predicting the future reactions and patterns of behavior of seminarians, as compared with collegians, has been prepared. It consists in measures of emotionality on the conscious as well as on the unconscious (physiological) levels. It also contains paper-and-pencil tests of feelings and attitudes toward life situations, and toward one's own ability to cope with the same. The fuller description of the tests will be given under the heading of methods. The collegians were 50 college students at a large mid-west Catholic university. They were all males, freshmen and sophomores, and about half were day-students, the other half boarders in the dormitory. The 50 seminarians were all residents at a large Roman Catholic Seminary in the mid-west, and they too were at the freshman or sophomore level.

Method

Subjects and Materials: The collegians and seminarians who made up the one hundred volunteers were all motivated to participate by means of a lecture by one of their professors. He stressed the fact that they would contribute to the cause of science by their efforts, and that therefore they must try to be honest, or else not take the tests, since they might otherwise be responsible for promulgating errors in science. All S's received by reason of their participation, the equivalent of one class credit for a course in psychology — about as much as the equivalent of one-fourth of a term paper. They all took the tests in the same order. This was the following: 1) Taylor Anxiety (modified), 2) Perseveration, 3) Loyola Language Study, 4) Neurological.

The Tests and Procedures: The modified Taylor Anxiety Scale was group administered, using IBM scoring methods. This yielded the "K" score, and four other factors which were extracted by Walker and Nicolay (1963) and designated as "M" or anxiety turned inward; "O" or anxiety outward; "P" or personal inadequacy; and MAS or general anxiety as defined by J. Taylor (Spence) et al. The "K" scale is generally taken to indicate the amount of "defensiveness" or tendency to fake good or bad, possessed by the subjects. If this is excessive it may invalidate the test. The "K" scale served as a safeguard against faulty test-taking attitudes. Reasons for using the Anxiety scale were that it would be a check on both the neurotic index (physiological) and on the LLS which used only "association" and not question-answer responses. It was suspected that the collegians might differ from the seminarians on one or the other of the four factors of the Anxiety scale, probably the one called personal inadequacy.

The Tests: Perseveration.

This test dates back to the days of W. Stephenson (1934) and R. B. Cattell (1936), but Weisgerber has done most to standardize the test for ideational perseveration (1951, 54, 55). This last author has published the results of his attempt to correlate the perseveration tendency (ideational) with recovery rate on the Psychogalvanic reflex. There was found to be a just barely reliable correlation: the slow recoverers were the high perseverators. The test measures the tendency to persist in one mode of thought (or action) in spite of a strong conscious effort to shift to a different mode. Weisgerber (1955) has factored the ideational test which he prepared, into four clusters designated by him as I, most probably a tendency to aimless perseveration, whether it be of images, ideas, or affective states; Factor II, sensory and imaginal impressions; Factor III, feeling and emotion; Factor IV, a tendency to worry and be anxious. Since both the high and low scores on this test have been considered undesirable (bad characters, according to Cattell), it will be interesting to try to evaluate the results of this study. The Perseveration scale was included in the battery so as to indicate possible character deficiencies along the lines of too much rigidity and/or too little adaptability or pliability, due to different early and school environments. It was surmised that the seminarians would be more submissive, adaptable, pliable, though not with enough assurance to use a one-tailed test for differences.

The Tests: The Loyola Language Study (LLS) (Herr, 1957, 66).

This test aims at evaluating mostly unconscious and involuntary patterns of thought and action. The Kent-Rosanoff Free Association Test on which it was based was a diagnostic tool used by psychiatrists in order to isolate bizarre and unusual modes of thinking. Subjects were asked to respond with the first word that came to mind, as quickly as possible. If the response given was "odd," or shared with only a small percentage of the general population taking the test, and if this "oddity" persisted throughout a large percentage of the 100 words which constituted the test, the respondent was definitely in need of psychiatric attention (Rosanoff, 1927). The creators of the LLS modified this procedure so that the instructions now read: "Read each of the stimulus words carefully, one by one, and after each one pause as long as you wish; try to judge which one word the majority of people would associate with it; take all the time you want but be sure to try to think out what most people would associate with this stimulus word; write down just this one response after the stimulus word." Thus the score for the total test will be taken to indicate "communality" of thought or some kind of empathy. It is definitely not a score for a sudden and unreflected "free" association: it is definitely not the same as would be obtained if the usual Kent-Rosanoff instructions had been given (Herr, 1957). The scores on the LLS do not correlate with intelligence or school grades, but do seem to indicate a social attitude or readiness to behave in a stereotyped manner (Stewart, 1963; Dinello, 1958; Lucinia, 1966). Other things being equal, poorer scores are made by older persons if education is kept constant. The trend extends up to ages 50 and 60 when education has likely ceased. Again, better scores are made by more educated persons, with age kept constant. The crucial fact is, however, that the test discriminates between mentally well-adjusted persons and schizophrenics, as judged by nurses and psychiatrists in the mental hospital. This explains in a preliminary way the reason for its inclusion in our present battery of tests. The LLS was also chosen in order to detect possible extreme cases of maladjustment and/or withdrawing tendencies, isolationism, unsociability, and the like. It had been used over a period of a dozen years in the screening of seminarians. Predictions were that seminarians would have more deviant scores than collegians, but in previous samples the differences were often insignificant. Other interpretations would be possible, namely that "loneliness" would tend to make the seminarians more deviant; this tendency to loneliness has been known to cause grave problems for seminarians in the past.

Note: The Perseveration and the LLS were taken individually at a single sitting followed by the Neurological.

The Tests: Neurological.

The next test was the psychogalvanometric test for neuroticism, prepared and distributed by Herr and Kobler (1953). This is basically a free-association test of the Kent-Rosanoff (1927) type, using specially selected emotionally-toned words as stimuli, while the neurological accompaniments (conductance changes) are being measured. The instrumental set-up was the same as that used in 1953 and 1956 save that only one apparatus was used for both groups. The galvanometer was a G-M, D'Arsonval Type, purchased in Chicago and described in their Series Catalogue, 570-600, Form 2316, pages 1 and 2. It has a period of four seconds, is highly sensitive and very rugged, and enables the experimenter to read a deflection of .06 microamperes per millimeter of scale. The photographic scale is 160 mm. distant from mirror. The scale is linear up to about 1500 ohms deflection, which is about the limit of the responses measured. The current flow is well below the threshold of conscious sensitivity. The bridge is of the closed type, and the coil is critically damped. The first arrangement causes the amount of current passing through the bridge to remain constant, and therefore that through all subjects is constant and *the same* when they are in balance, no matter what their basic conductance might be. The second factor prevents the moving coil from swinging freely, that is, without any real changes in conductance. These points are of very great importance these days when the current-density per unit area of electrode must be controlled. The current was applied through anodized pure silver electrodes, applied to the first and third finger, through a specially prepared electrode jelly. This was recommended to the writer by Biophysical Research Instruments, Inc., by letter in fall 1964. The paste is equivalent to a NaCl buffer solution, but its density prevents drying, and results in constant current flow regardless of small changes in finger position. Photographic timing was secured by means of synchronous motors supplied by Merkle-Korff of Chicago.

Each S, after cleansing hands, took his seat in the apparatus and was balanced and listened to instructions during a five minute adaptation period. This might vary a few minutes depending upon the amount of variability of the S, and then a few stimuli were given on a trial basis, a deep breath was taken, and then the regular list of words was begun. The E could visually monitor the movements of the indicator, and took care to see that no deflections were allowed to go off the record, and that S had fully recovered from one stimulus before another was given. Key signals were placed on the record at the time of stimulus, at the time of verbal response; both these signal dots were doubly indicated on the record by means of a special serial arrangement of the lighting circuit thus giving E a *double* check on the reaction time.

The free-association to eight words (with the buffer words between them) was followed by a brief pause in which the S moved about freely — having been seated in a fixed but relaxed position for some 10-15 minutes; then the second half of the words was given. After this was a pause during which the S, without being disconnected from the instrument, read silently from a constant speed memory drum, a specially prepared threatening essay.[1] Finally the crucial part of the procedure was this: Five of the most emotional words; namely love, fear, shame, sin and self, were presented a second time, in the same order as before, with recordings and conditions of measurements exactly the same as before the essay. It should be remembered that during the whole session the subject's general adaptation level, as well as all spontaneous and "specially stimulated" EDRs were being continuously measured. These two variables, namely, the basic conductance level and the momentary EDRs, are totally dependent upon each other since the same identical electrical hook-up records them. In order to understand the interpretation of results later on, we repeat: Those two measures, though statistically independent — are electrically totally dependent upon each other. This must be stressed over and over. The slow changes in basic conductances, called at the present time by most writers the adaptation or background level, is one variable. Another is the rapid momentary changes superimposed upon the former. They are usually designated electrodermal response, (or GSR). Ax gives the precise definition of these as changes of at least 3 micromhos per second, in the basic conductance. In more

---

1. The essays are found in Appendix VI.

concrete and practical terms, the EDRs begin their course and end the same in about 20 to 40 seconds, depending upon their amplitudes. Slow changes in background may require as much as five minutes to change one micromho.

Reaction times, both for the verbal and for the electrodermal responses were measured to a fraction of a second. The advantages of this set-up are obvious when one remembers that there will be needed for the interpretation both a measure of the rate of change of conductance, and the duration and extent of the same.

The total testing time on the EDR ran between 25 and 45 minutes with an average of 36. Ss were immediately warned not to speak to others about the experiment. This was in order to keep information uniform. Ss were told the value of the experiment would be lost if they violated this instruction, and that in so doing they might be injuring the cause of science. They generously promised to conform, and it appears they kept their promises. They all agreed that the neurological part of the experiment was the most interesting part of the battery.

We shall come back to the units of measurement used in the treatment of results. Here let it be said that derived scores have been computed for each of the subjects in each group, for each of the pre-stress GSRs, for the 5-minute period of stress, and for the post-stress GSRs of five words. Each of these measures involved both the "amount and rate of deflection" and the basic or background conductances. At this point we may say that the transformations that proved most useful for the statistical treatment of the data were the log-changes-in-conductance and the Haggard transformation (see Montague and Coles, 1966). This latter was defined as the log-change-in-resistance (or conductance if we use cologs) minus a constant empirically determined, divided by the resistance at the start of deflection. Both these transformations yielded distributions in which the score was independent (statistically) of the background, and the units were equal throughout the whole range of scores — also the criterion of homogeneity of variances was met.

The reasons for including the EDR test are obvious, but most importantly the researcher wished to determine to what extent neurotic persons tend to enter the seminary rather than remain in the world of non-religious avocations. Predictions on the basis of much previous work in this field were that there would be no difference from group to group, and that the college group would also be within the normal range. Other reasons were that the project wished to measure stress, and the ability of the two groups to withstand stress, especially if indicators were found over which the Ss had no possibility of conscious control. We shall see later that for scores on the test taken as a whole, there were slight but not significant differences. When the test was broken down item by item, certain parts of the battery did show highly significant differences between the two groups, notably on their ability to withstand stress when stimulated with notions of "shame." To the writer's surprise there were absolutely no inter-group differences, either in the pre- or in the post-test situation, in responsiveness to fear, to sin, to shame, love or to one's own self. Actually, however, both groups showed much more reactivity (conductivity) after the stress than before. The significant differences for pre-compared to post-stress were for collegians on the words love, fear, and sin; whereas they were for the seminarians on the words love, sin, ashamed, and self. In all cases the differences were in the same direction, more reactivity. In all these comparisons, since the same Ss were used before and after the threats, the t-test for correlated means was used, although the actual correlations turned out to be zero, and this seems to show a heightening differential effect of the threats — they acted differently on the same people involved with them.

The prediction made in the design of the experiment was that collegians and seminarians would react very differently to stress, owing to the fact that collegians are in constant danger of the draft and the seminarians are not, so long as they remain in their seminary. Pehaps the seminarians, like the collegians, are in somewhat the same predicament, because they have both the risk of "poor grades" and then draft; obviously they would not be allowed to stay in the seminary, just as they would not likely remain in college, if their grades were to deteriorate.

Methods of Analysis

In general, wherever the data warranted it, analysis of variance was used. Otherwise, simple *t*-tests in two variables had to suffice. Correlational techniques were used because it was thought that there would be closer clustering of scores for one group than for the other. About half of the time this prediction was verified, and this will be the main task of our analysis of results, the attempt to find out why there is this difference. Another reason for running the correlations is the prediction that there would be some rather close connections between the various tests of functions operating on the unconscious level, namely the neurological, the LLS, and certain parts of the anxiety test. On the other hand, paper-and-pencil tests probably will be expected to correlate highly with each other. The conscious and the unconscious, probably, would be related to about zero with each other. The higher the correlation between the conscious and the unconscious functions, the more highly the groups would be integrated, it was hypothesized. Under results we shall come back to this point.

All the data were processed by a representative of the Loyola Data Processing Department, for the possibility of utilizing the university's 1401 computer, and the cards were subsequently punched, so as to find the significance of the difference between the two groups on all tests, as well as to correlate each test with every other one. As it turned out, much of the calculation had to be done by hand because of shortage of help in the data processing center. And the other scores were all spot-checked so as to be able to make uniform judgments about the results.

Results

There were two experimental groups of 46 each participating in the experiment. One called group A consisted of collegians, and the other, group B of seminarians. There were nine main variables that were compared, namely perseveration, empathy, neuroticism partial, neuroticism total, internal anxiety, external anxiety, personal inadequacy, general anxiety, and defensiveness.

A tabular arrangement (Table 1A, appendix II) of these nine scores for each of the two groups will illustrate the essential similarity between them. Details of such difference will be given later.

Sub-total scores were computed for several of the tests, and the result will be given later under analyses of variance. The crux of the experiment was to compare the scores before the threatening instructions on the EDR (GSR), and those during the threat, and both with those after the threatening instructions, with five of the previous stimuli being repeated; the purpose of this arrangement, it will be remembered, was to compare the reactiveness of the two groups to these very disturbing instructions. The instructions will be summarized in appendix VI. The similarities and differences will be discussed and evaluated after the other analyses of variance are analyzed in separate pages. In the concluding paragraphs the common trends shown by the two groups during the whole neurological test will be described, as well as some individual differences between every eighth seminarian and every eighth collegian, when these are arranged in alphabetical order.

The reader is again reminded that an analysis of variance was run using all 92 subjects and all 19 EDR (of GSR) stimuli before the threat. This proved highly significant and so a *t*-test could be run between each pair of words. Similarly an analysis was run for each group of 46 taken separately, using interaction as the error term. This confirmed the conclusion that significant differences were to be found at least in some parts of the items of the tests. These analyses were so highly significant that they are not shown in tabular form.

THE CORRELATIONS

The first thing that strikes one upon scanning the correlation matrix (appendix I) for the nine variables, each correlated with each other, is the fact that in the majority of the cases, those for the seminarians are higher than those for the collegians. This might be taken to mean that the battery as a whole reveals greater consistency of inner personality structure for the former than for the latter. One could push the same thinking further and ask whether or not the relationship between the unconscious qualities and the conscious ones, as measured by the various tests, would be stronger for the seminarians than for the collegians.

The workers have attempted to do just that. They have already designated three tests as measuring qualities over which the subject has no conscious control, namely the Loyola Language Study, the Neurological partial and the Neurological total. They now consider each one of these separately, and compute the average correlation which it has with the six tests which measure conscious qualities. At least the other six require a yes-no type of answer and it may be assumed that these answers were deliberately given by each of the Ss. The average of the correlations, regardless of sign, is used, since negative correlations as well as positive ones indicate a degree of going-togetherness. With the LLS the average r for the seminarians was .053 and that for the collegians was .094. Obviously none of these is significant and all together can only be taken to indicate trends. But still, by our criterion of magnitude of correlation between tests of conscious traits, and those which tap the unconscious, the collegians are the more integrated.

The average correlation, regardless of sign, between neurological total and the other six is .125 for the seminarians and .150 for the collegians. That for neurological partial with the other six is .082 for the seminarians and .230 for the collegians. Among those for neurological total only that with anxiety-outwards was significant at the .01 level. Among those for neurological partial two were significant at the .05 level, namely those with anxiety-in and with "K." These averages are only slightly changed by throwing in both the two other tests of unconscious traits so as to average each of the three with all the other eight instead of the other six.

Hence the analysis up to now would seem to favor the collegians as being the better integrated. But it must be remembered that few, if any, of the individual correlations, are large enough to make a certain judgment, that they could not have been due to chance. That is, they are not sufficient to make predictions that are capable of being replicated with frequencies much more than chance. They were not significant at the .05 level, much less the .01.

Now the paper-and-pencil type will be considered. The first is that for Perseveration. As said before this is an indicator of healthy flexibility of character; and from it we would expect that the well-integrated person would score in the middle; both extremes are considered unstable. In the middle range are found persons whose conscious impulses to continue in certain habits which are once begun, will correlate highly with their other conscious impulses. Hence correlations were sought between perseveration scores and all the anxiety factors; thus there is one score, namely perseveration, which is correlated with each of five others, namely anxiety-in, anxiety-out, personal inadequacy, "K," and general anxiety. The correlations are, first for seminarians, then for collegians, .529 and .469; .517 and .350; .530 and .295 — .590 and — .327; .628 and .333; giving an average of .559 for seminarians and .355 for collegians. These correlations are significantly different from each other at the .01 level, and all in favor of the seminarians. So by taking the relationship of the conscious factors among each other, the advantage is on the side of the seminarians.

Finally, if one were to take *only* those two variables, namely perseveration and general anxiety, which account for 18 out of all the 32 significant correlations, and average them, seminarians are far ahead of collegians in consistency. Even in the other 14 cells not comparing these two traits, the average for the seminarians is .593 and that for collegians is .393, which is about the same difference.

There remains the consideration of the fairly consistent negative correlations with the "K" factor. The interpretation made by some Minnesota Multiphasic Inventory users is the following: High scores on this variable indicate either too much defensiveness, or too much openness and strictness in answering the other questions. Since none of the mean anxiety factors discriminate the seminarians from the collegians, it is not very likely that the "K" is an exception. There is a very consistent negative correlation between "K" and the M, O, P, and MAS anxiety factors. Since this correlation is always higher for the seminarians than for the collegians, and reliably so, it might possibly mean that the former are more open in their attitude toward the test, as well as more consistent throughout.

The Difference Between Means: The Perseveration Test

The Perseveration test discriminated between the two groups with the seminarians on the lower side. Since the test may be looked upon as estimating a tendency to find difficulty in voluntarily changing a habit or behavior pattern once begun, high scores may be looked upon sometimes as desirable and again as undesirable. It would all depend upon the kind of habit that was being discussed. Most of the questions on the test seem to have involved consciously developed desirable habits, but others might have referred to involuntary automatic patterns of thought and action. None of them made reference to morally or socially undesirable habits. Hence the differences between the two groups would seem to mean that there was somewhat less rigidity, in general, among the seminarians; possibly even more flexibility, adaptability and readiness for new experiences. They would seem to need such readiness in the strenuous life of training which they have chosen for themselves. Again *no* individuals were so extreme in their scores (2 S.D.s from mean) as to make them bad characters, whether on the fixity, stubbornness end of the scale (high perseverators) or on the fluidity, changeability, wishywashy end.

The Neurological Tests, partial and total

It was stated in the section on methods (page 109) that Haggard transformations were computed for each single response to each stimulus. These were further manipulated in order to secure a neurotic index (Herr, Kobler, 1957). This was simply the ratio of the mean of 5 neurotic words to the mean of 4 normal words, as measured for each subject. This ratio is called the partial score. The mean for all 19 words per each S is the total score.

There were no intergroup differences on either of these two scores. The differences were slight, about just equal to chance differences. In both partial and total scores the direction of differences was toward more neural involvement for the seminarians. This test was selected for the precise purpose of weeding out bad risks from a neurological point of view. Two individuals among the collegians reached the danger point of 2 S.D.s beyond the mean and two of the seminarians. One of these latter had of his own accord told the tester that he was undergoing counselling because of nervousness and strain.

Any person whose neurotic index was 2 S.D.s above the mean, would even be considered a bad risk for college, as shown in a Loyola study; and hence, it may be argued, also for the seminary in which the strenuous training over a long period of time has often been compared to the military.

The changes in pre-stress compared to the post-stress responses on the neurological will be treated under separate headings.

The LLS was significantly different for the two groups and the seminarians were less empathetic, had less communality than the collegians. It may be easy to see why they might not know so well as collegians do, what most other people their age would think and say in response to the eighty words on the test. This is so because many or even most of them have been prone to look upon themselves from earliest childhood as persons set apart, that is, dedicated to the service of God. As such, they might even have been trained to think in ways which are quite different from the "ways of the world"; if the communality score really indicates a lesser degree of "feeling" with the rest of the world, perhaps in a certain sense this is desirable also. It is to be hoped that the feeling tones of the seminarians in preparation for the ministry are not too far removed from those of the "people of God" whom they prepare to serve by their long years in the seminary.

Again it is to be noted that both group-means were well within the normal range of scores. Among seminarians two individuals were on dangerous extremes, one of whom had misread the instructions and thus probably invalidated his score; and the other was found, on a follow-up interview, to be leaving the seminary and seeking help.

The Analyses of Variance

Those tests which permitted quantitative scoring of the various items, namely the LLS and the neurological, were subjected to several analyses of variance, in order to determine the sources of variance among the items, individually or in groups, the persons, and between the two groups of persons.

The first was a two-factor experiment with repeated measures in factor B.[2] This was a 2 by 2 by 10 run on the ten most discriminating items of the LLS. Five of the words were self-oriented in meaning and the other five were not. One might have guessed that the seminarians were more self-regarding than the collegians and hence would score more highly on these five words (appendix II, Table 1B).

In analysis A, collegians' means were compared to those for seminarians, for all the ten words, and there was no difference; however, in the breakdown by individual words (taking interaction of words by within groups as error term), there is a highly significant F. The word "bread" has poorer scores for collegians whereas "table" and "stomach" have poorer scores for seminarians.

In analysis B, the mean for the "Self" words was compared to that for the "Object" words, and there was no significant difference for either group of persons.

The second analysis was on the neurological scores, prior to

---

2. Cf. Winer, 1962, **Statistical Principles in Experimental Design**, p. 218.

the stress instructions. Nineteen stimuli were used, as stated above in a simple two-way analysis, in order to learn whether or not some words would add more than others to the discriminatory power of the test, and perhaps differently for the two groups. From this also a quick estimate of the standard error of any mean was reached.[3] In this two-way test the F was highly significant, and a difference of .89 was found to be needed in order to distinguish one word-response from another. The words "church" and "God" showed collegians more neurologic; the word "breast" made the seminarians more neurologic, according to this single type of indicator, of course.

A third analysis was run as a check on the first, but with three factors, namely the 19 words, the 46 persons, the interaction. Again the F values were highly significant, using the interaction as the error term. Those had to be run separately for the seminarians and the collegians, and here it is possible to notice the great difference in the total variances of the two groups. This could have been noticed also by a careful study of the means and standard deviations of each of the nine major items of the test battery. Seminarians were higher on the average only on neurological total. Just what it means is not altogether clear, since one might rather have surmised that the seminarians as a group would be more homogeneous than the collegians even on the neurological level.

The fourth analysis is the *heart* of the whole research, since it treats of the comparison between the pre-threat scores and the post-threat scores for both the collegians and the seminarians. This was possible on only a few of the neurological items, since only they were repeated as stimuli for the EDR after the threatening instruction. These words were love, fear, sin, shame, and self. This was a 2 by 2 by 5 factorial, with repeated measures in the last two factors. It aimed at evaluating the variances due

---

3. Cf. Lindguist, Everet F., Statistical analysis in Educational Research, N.Y. Houghton Mifflin, 1940.

to seminarians versus collegians (Factor A), threatening versus non-threatening instructions (Factor B), and the words used before and after threat to evoke EDR (Factor C). In this case the Factors B and C were significant beyond the .01 level. In addition there was a significant interaction. But the Between Subjects Factor was not significant. It was only after the various relationships had been plotted, and looked upon with respect to the original data that an interpretation was possible with regard to the interaction. It was very probably due to the transformation of scores used. It means that when the scores *after* involvement are considered (condition b2), they are so shrunken (actually heightened in autonomic activity) that it takes bigger differences to become significant; whereas before the threatening instructions (condition b1) there are much larger differences in score, both between the two groups of persons and between the non-threat and threatening conditions. As a result of the t-tests for the differences between seminarians and collegians before and after the threat, few were found to approach the .05 level; they were the words "love" and "fear" for the condition before, and the word "ashamed" for the condition after.

However, when t-tests were run for the conditions b1 and b2 we have a different story. Seminarians before the threat, compared to seminarians after, on four words were different; namely "love," "ashamed," "sin," and "self"; collegians before, compared to after, differed on three words; namely "love," "afraid," and "sin"; and the differences were all in the same direction, namely more reactivity after. Notice that "love" and "sin" were only two words common to both groups; and that seminarians were more "ego-involved."

TOTAL COURSE OF NEROLOGICAL TESTS

Lastly but not leastly, the two groups of persons will be compared as to the whole course of conductance changes from beginning to end of the neurological tests. Figure 1 Appendix III shows the seminarians' and the collegians' conductances sampled over 3 pre-threat words, 3 stages during the threat, and 2 post-threat words. This is an average of all 46 subjects on each of the stimuli.

Figure 2 shows 6 seminarians, that is, every seventh one in alphabetical order in the same situations as were described above for the averages for each of the two groups.

Figure 3 shows 6 collegians, that is, every seventh one in alphabetical order in the same situations as were described above for the averages for each of the two groups.

DISCUSSION OF RESULTS

1) The differences between seminarians and collegians are mainly in the three tests called empathy (LLS), perseveration, and defensiveness. Cutting points can be established whereby the counsellor or guidance person would be able to make recommendations as to whether the person tested should or should not go into the seminary. Any score above 701 on the empathy (LLS) test (which would be two standard deviations off the mean), or one above 62.0 on the perseveration test (again 2 S.D.s off), would mean a poor risk. Also a "K" or defensiveness score more than 26.0 would probably mean a poor risk, although the interpretation of this test is subject to much controversy.

2) The neurological partial test is useful, as it always has been in the past, in discriminating the grossly neurotic. He would score on or above 1.72 on the neurological ratio score (The Herr-Kobler (1957) index).

3) Since four words, namely love, sin, shame, and self give significantly higher responses on the galvanometer after the threatening instructions than before them, the cutting point of 2 S.D.s would again be a good guide for judging persons unfit, from a neurological point of view. The score values, using

Haggard scores, would be 712, 591, 677 and 645 respectively. Also since three words on the empathy test discriminated seminarians from collegians, these could also be used as a counter check upon the neurological tests above mentioned. The seminarian who would score a 35 for the word "table," or 35 for "stomach," or 38 for "bread" should be carefully scrutinized, and all the more so if all three were high.

4) The means and S.D.s for the neurological total should also be used diagnostically, even though they do not discriminate seminarians from collegians. Any average EDR score (Haggard transformation) of 670 or over would look suspicious, especially in combination with the other indicators mentioned above.

5) Similar interpretations may be given to the Taylor Anxiety and the three sub-tests. For the total MAS a score of 30 is in need of attention, all the more so if corroborated by results of the neurological tests. On the sub-test internal anxiety, a score on or above 18; for external anxiety one on or above 16; and for the personal inadequacy, one of 19 would be crucial.

6) The total progression in the trend of the skin conductance changes for each subject, as he sits through the neurological association test, should be graphed. It may then be compared to similar curves for the individual seminarians (very stable) and collegians (very variable — see figures). If the person being tested showed extreme deviations from a central trend he should probably be considered a poor risk.

A word must be said about the conditions for administering and interpreting the test battery. The utmost care should be taken in seeing that the subjects all receive the same instructions. If these are not followed exactly no valid predictions can be made. In the case of the study just described, they were tape recorded for the crucial parts of the battery, namely the EDR studies using free association as the medium. Here it must be emphasized that if the tester should ever fail to put in this one phrase "as quickly as possible" no one can predict the consequences. And again, in case the subjects did not understand that, in the case of the LLS or the empathy test, they need *not* respond with the first thing that comes to mind, that is *not respond as quickly as possible,* altogether different results will be obtained. We have ample experimental evidence for these remarks, gathered over a period of some 20 years. So the meaning is clear now, it is hoped, about the overwhelming requirement of *"proper instructions."*

As for the psychogalvanometer and recorder, these are the two main items for which special training is needed. Suitable equipment may now be obtained for reasonable cost, but experience and supervision are the only methods for mastering the technique. All the other tests are paper-and-pencil tests, but again the importance must be stressed of seeing that all Ss know and follow instructions. Facilities are available at the author's research laboratory, for machine scoring of most of the test material, as well as for data processing. Any interested researcher could easily make arrangement with the author for administering and scoring the test battery. In some cases the cost might be defrayed by reason of grants to the department here at Loyola. In others, modest fees would be charged.

Those parts of the battery which seem, at this point, to be in need of cross validation, are the perseveration test, and the effect of the threatening instructions on the course of conductivity changes mediated by the autonomic nervous system. These areas are constantly being explored at Loyola, and with the aid of interested colleagues and graduate assistants. At this point there is no hesitation on our part in affirming that the neurotic index, perfected by Herr and Kobler as a discriminator of neurotic tendency over the last 15 years, will hold up, if the tests are properly administered. Secondly, the threatening instructions which for safety purposes are in an Appendix, or some modification of them have been successfully employed by others in producing startling changes in the conductivity of the skin, under the EDR tests of autonomic activity. Lazarus and his team, et al. (1962), have been constantly calling this to our attention. The pattern of behavior change is not a spurious one. But it is not one that lends itself to any pat or easy interpretation.

APPLICATIONS FOR THE USE OF COUNSELORS AND STUDENTS

The reader may have been wondering what he will be able to do, after reading these pages. We shall try to lay down some rules, as also some precautions to guide him. Of course the guides will differ very much in cases of the different tests.

For the perseveration test and Thorne's self-audit, less preparation is needed on the part of the tester. The author and his associates will be able to supply all the tests from Loyola, if and when it is judged that the counsellor or guidance worker who asks for them, is entitled to use them.

The Rice-LeSenne-Berger test of temperament differs from the original. The name "Rice" is used, because he has with great pains revised the original English translation completely as to grammar. These several tests must be sent to Loyola for scoring since they are in experimental stages. Should one wish to use any of them, it would greatly facilitate matters if he were to get in touch with the author at Loyola, and come to some conclusions as to methods before starting on a project of such an importance as personality testing.

It is highly recommended that, before any person takes upon himself the burden of testing others, in regard to their adjustment quality, or the character of their other emotional tendencies he consults with competent authorities in the field. Let him remember that this is not a matter to be undertaken lightly. Samples of tests, which are in the experimental stage, are given in the Appendices. They are placed here mainly in order that the reader may better understand the matter discussed in the text. The oldest and most widely used one seems to be the Rice test. It is widely used, especially in Canada, and in foreign countries. As stated before, it gives a measure of three main and eight subsidiary traits. But for the best results, some trained psychologist-counsellor (or other skilled person), ought to be called in for the interpretation. This rule holds especially when there is question of the emotional and volitional side of one's personality and character. If *problems* appear which center around the deepest inner secrets of the conscience of the person, let him then not cease to find a trusted and competent adviser. In this person he should place implicit and total confidence, because according to an ancient proverb: "No man is a good judge in his own cause." The seriousness of the responsibility residing in the tester cannot be overestimated.

The MMPI is a standardized test, for the purpose of evaluating personality from the psychiatric point of view. Persons desiring to use this test must get in touch with a trained clinical psychologist. If they should desire the services of the Loyola Services Center, they should get in touch with either the director of the Psychological Clinic or with the director of the Psychological Services Center and Guidance Clinic.

Now to return to the Loyola Battery of tests, which was perfected, tested, and revised over a period of some ten years. Most of these were used on the college population; others were used on the thirteen or more major seminaries that are in the neighborhood of Chicago. The reason they are not the so-called standardized tests which claim so much attention on the general market, is that they have not been used on a population covering the nation. The Loyola Language is one test which has been so standardized, by means of years of painstaking research. And many of the items on the perseveration test have been used on countless subjects. And the items have not been substantially changed, down the ages. Scoring systems used have varied, owing to a tendency for distributions to be skewed, and the fact that correlations with other tests tend to be curvilinear.

Again, the reader is reminded that great caution must be used in taking the tests. For instance, should a given person have previously seen the scoring system for the items of either test, then he must by no means ever take that test himself. It would be a sheer waste of time and besides it would lead to the most absurd consequences. Let this serve as a caution, once and for all. It would seem that the reason in back of this precaution would be totally or at least mostly clear to any rational and sensible person.

The Loyola Language Study is, as was stated, both validated and standardized for the United States. It has separate forms, for men and for women, since at the very beginning of the research with this tool, it was obvious that the kind of associations given by men were totally different than those given by women.

Since this test purports to discriminate neurotics from normals in the general population, it is obvious that the scoring norms may not be published at all. Should a person, here or there, think that he has found out the meaning of such scores, he ought to consult the author who will initiate him into the secrets of the scoring system.

The Walker-Nicolay-Taylor anxiety scale is not found in the Appendix, since it is currently being revised. In general, the meaning of the scores, in the case of the Perseveration, Anxiety and Language Study, is determined by the extent to which a person deviates from the average of a group (assuming honest answers), in the kind of answers he chooses to give to the various questions. Of course, this system of scoring is always comparative, as it must be when norms are sought.

Finally the Depth test of neuroticism, the Electrodermal response, requires an instrumental set-up. The psychology department at Loyola University, as well as many other universities, is equipped to administer the emotional stimulus words, and to record the magnitude and duration of the autonomic responses of the nervous system.

Yet here too, unless the method of administration used at Loyola were to be followed in all its exactness, comparable results could not be expected. Seriously interested parties may contact, by phone or by mail, the author of this book or one of his assistants. Arrangements can be had for a cooperative enterprise between qualified experimenters and the Loyola staff.

It is not necessary that the Loyola battery always be given in its entirety. The parts which would be deemed sufficient, in particular cases, might be as few as two or three. Moreover, should the results of some one particular test be extremely deviant, then more thorough probing would be found necessary. One last remark needs to be made here, and it is with regard to the possibility of repeated testing. It is quite obvious that the tests used for suiting a person to his job, can also be of much use in the "follow-up" process. No one remains immutable, as he goes through the experiences of life. Changes can also be induced by reason of the fact that information often leaks out about the tests and hence the norms once established become invalid and so does the subsequent interpretation. Again no two cases are identical, and a safe rule to follow is to choose the adviser who is as qualified as possible,to speak with respect to the problems which arise and the subsequent solutions.

SUGGESTIONS FOR FURTHER RESEARCH

The Vatican Council had some very pertinent deliberations, with regard to this whole question of seminary tests and training. It arrived at some conclusions which are very much in line with the present author's findings. One needs to remember that it was also consonant with the general aims of the Council, that many faiths should collaborate in their general effort to renew the work of the Church and its ministers, for the people of God throughout the world. Stated slightly differently, the aims of the Council would best be served if people of many faiths should engage in frequent and serious dialogues, by means of which all peoples should be brought into closer union with one another and with their Creator.

One of the most active and influential participants in the Council, as everyone knows, was Cardinal Bea. He has recently published a book on the Hebraeo-Christian relations, in the past and right up to the present. This one single publication seems to have stimulated a great amount of research in the area of Old and New Testament Studies. Especially has the Eminent Cardinal been responsible for changes in the liturgy that might have affected very crucially and vitally the relationships, both ancient and recent, between Christians and Jews. In other words he has been a pillar of strength in the whole ecumenical movement. His work was one of the factors in bringing a great variety of consultants to attend parts of the Council, including the present author.

While in Rome it was possible for the author to arrange not only for daily visits to the Council meetings of the Third Session, but also to the special press staff conferences, with representatives of the press from all parts of the world. At these latter sessions, another member of Loyola University faculty, Rev. Charles A. Curran, then a peritus for the Council in the area of seminary curricula, helped make known the aims of Loyola's updated post-graduate training program for the clergy of the Chicago area. It was at these two meetings that Fr. Curran and the present author planned a still further stage of the ecumenical program. As all know, the Vatican has its own privately operated Radio Broadcast System. Its representative at the Council then approached the author and asked him for an interview over the Vatican International Radio, on the two projects most dear to the Cardinal mentioned above, and to Fr. Curran. These two were the movement to update the curriculum in seminaries, making it meet the needs of the times more efficiently; and to spread the ecumenical movement as widely as possible, so as to take in its scope the findings of other religious denominations, in the broader area of the relation between religion and mental health, so far as the special function of the clergy is concerned. For it is this role which gives them a part in the great humanitarian work of maintaining the health of the people, physical as well as mental. Naturally if the role of the clergy were to be made clear from earliest days of the seminary, their ability to help prevent mental illness as well as to work effectively on teams of experts who treat the same, would be enhanced. Then the seminaries would also have to recognize this fact and to start planning their training accordingly.

It was these experiences in Rome in the autumn of 1965 which stimulated the author and his team of researchers to continue the study of the actual status of affairs as existing today in America. Such a study includes the constant evaluation of the seminarians' training, in key seminaries which were used in the original NIMH-supported Project of Loyola University, in cooperation with Harvard and Yeshiva. But particularly it includes that part of the program which tried to evaluate the efficacy of Catholic Seminary training, in preserving mental health. In other words the goal of the on-going research now widens so as to include continuous evaluation, from many angles, of the kind of training Catholic Seminarians receive, so far as the mental health aspects are concerned. A very recent project has been initiated which involves the measure of patterns of brain waves, in relation to induced stress. This promises to be a very revealing approach.

Again, the evaluation of the training aspect was and still is one of the major contributions which Loyola is making, in collaboration with Harvard and Yeshiva. The goals of all three schools' programs are first of all to evaluate the seminary curricula for all faiths, in terms of their serving the public by training ministers to use their special function as ministers, in the overall mental health of the nation. Secondarily they are to update the training which ministers of all faiths receive, in terms of their efficacy in reaching these goals.

As is known, the three Universities received a total of almost half a million over a period from 1955 through 1961 for the precise purpose of making this investigation. All three schools were told that this was a pilot study, to be continued through University and other support indefinitely. It is interesting to observe how closely the work of these three schools resembles some of the fact-finding procedures of Vatican II extending from 1964 onward. In fact, several of the topics that were so ably handled at the Council had actually been prepared by the workers on Seminary curricula in America.

With these remarks it will not be difficult to infer what the subject matter of the dialogue-interview over the Vatican Radio would be, back on that memorable evening (Rome) of Oct. 28, 1965. The summary of the dialogue follows after which several comments, imaging the reactions of the public, will be in order. (For summary of the Project, Cf., Herr, 1962, 1966).

It is the hope of the research team connected with the

NIMH Project at Loyola University that they may be able to aid ministers and other religious in gaining the prudence, wisdom and insight that can be afforded through the positive values of the modern behavioral sciences. A step forward will be made if there can be created in the minds of scientists and laymen an atmosphere which is more favorable to a better cooperation between theologians and therapists, between humanists and scientists. It is one thing to moralize and to be zealous in toiling for the mental and moral uplift of human beings; it is another to do these things without detriment to the individuals' overall happiness and well-being. Similarly, it is one thing for the scientist to assist and understand men's behavior by means of mental health principles, but is quite another to do these things in such a way that the highest interests and values of man, created in the image and likeness of God, can be maintained.

The Loyola Seminary Project agrees entirely with the opinions expressed by the workers at Harvard and Yeshiva, on this crucial point, namely, that the sciences of human behavior, including psychiatry, must give the utmost attention to the emotional maturity and growth of the prospective priest, Rabbi or minister. Thus, priests can be more open-minded and come to recognize the value for religion in the scientific study of the deeper dynamics of moral and religious growth. Likewise, conscientious workers in the field of science and psychiatry can become more broadminded and realize that religion and theology have some valid contributions to make toward enhancing the total sum of happiness of human beings. Scientists will not benefit humanity generally by claiming that religion is merely the "opium of the masses," or as analysts might do, saying that it is an "escape" into a mystical world of unreality.

The Loyola Project moves along cautiously, with the preparation of course materials for the various levels of seminary training, in line with the mental health needs of the individual students. Specific needs on three main levels of training are recognized: They are on the level of young trainees just entering upon their seminary life; then on the level of students ready for ordination; and finally, on the level of ordained priests who have actually begun their work of teaching, guidance and administration of the sacraments.

Seminary administrators, especially, are not unaware of the fact that an adequate training of priests for the ministry, while safeguarding mental health, will also give the trainees ample opportunity for self-actualization of their human potential and for realizing their highest spiritual goals.

At the end of the dialogue-interview the actual accomplishments of the Seminary Project, up to that day in the fall of 1965 were summarized as follows: Several larger seminaries have introduced new courses, as well as required visits to mental hospitals; during these weekly visits at the higher levels of training, the students would spend the whole day, mornings hearing lectures at the hospital, afternoons visiting the wards and engaging in seminar discussion on the relation of religion and mental health, with all the workers concerned, that is, psychiatrists, social works and psychiatric nurses. Other seminaries introduced "chairs" of religious psychology into their actual seminary curricula, and placed the appropriate professors on their staffs. Still other seminaries, farther removed from the larger cities, began sending their students, both philosophers and theologians, into social agencies during the summer months of vacation. All of them were thinking seriously, during their annual Rectors' meeting at the National Educational Associations's meetings, of ways in which the materials, sent them by the Loyola Project workers, might be more successfully and effectively applied. Of course, in the very recent past so many radical changes in seminary establishments have been made that it is impossible to summarize them.

In retrospect, the most striking findings of the Project were two: First, the fact that a screening process was not only necessary but also desired, by most of the seminary heads that were contacted. Secondly, the fact that the administrators were so very ready and eager to "put into practice" any and all findings of the research, provided that their effectiveness had been scientifically and reliably demonstrated to the satisfaction of the deans and presidents. Two other unexpected findings were those mentioned at the beginning of the talk on Vatican Radio: First, the needs of the beginners (ages 18 about) were predominantly self-centered, whereas those of the seniors (ages 23 about) were altero-centered. This meant that the near-graduates, that is those who were almost ready for ordination and the active pastoral life, had to be treated in a special way different from that of the novices. Stated in another way, those devoted and even dedicated young men who had just begun their training for assuming the role of mediator between God and the people of God, had to overcome their own personal difficulties, to settle their own deep-seated emotional problems before they could feel that they were suited for their vocation. This is what common sense would have told us, but we were still quite surprised to find the universality with which the study proved the fact.

On the other hand, those who had persevered in their training for six or eight years, now turned their attention to the external world, to check their own aspirations against the demands of the "Law," to see if their own preparation gave them real competence in handling the problems of others; in acting as true ministers of the Gospel, as effective mediators between God and man.

Although this whole problem of seminary curricular planning bristles with difficulty and much progress is being made through counsel and experimentation, the author and his staff surmise that the "nature" of man does not change radically down through the ages. Too much treatment of seminarians as "children" may have taken place in the past, thus giving rise to the fact that psychiatrists and such learned scientific persons call them "immature." Yet no known device seems available to this author, after covering the fields of literature in several fields of science, whereby egocentric youth and adolescent boys will bud forth suddenly, in the early years of seminary training, into mature adult socio-centric workers in the vineyard of the Lord, for the benefit of all the so-called enlightened people of God.

APPENDIX I

Correlation Matrix in Nine Variables
(Each with each other)
36 for collegians, 36 for seminarians, 72 total

	Perseveration	LLS	Neurolog. Partial	M	O	P	K	MAS	Neurolog. Total
	Col / Sem	Col / Sem	Col / Sem	Col / Sem	Col / Sem	Col / Sem	Col / Sem	Col / Sem	Col / Sem
Perseveration	X								
LLS	145 / -030	X							
Neurolog. Partial	072 / 006	060 / -102	X						
M	469 / 529	125 / -060	338 / 065	X					
O	350 / 517	115 / 006	227 / 077	401 / 462	X				
P	295 / 530	050 / 020	260 / -174	396 / 505	453 / 624	X			
K	-327 / -590	-116 / 188	-302 / 132	-389 / -668	-243 / -585	-142 / -713	X		
MAS	333 / 628	016 / 012	183 / 036	525 / 753	735 / 732	653 / 702	-486 / -657	X	
Neurolog. Total	006 / -117	143 / 227	437 / 047	151 / -078	431 / 033	146 / -256	-121 / -060	046 / -205	X

Need for significance at .01 level 376 (for N 46)
Need for significance at .05 level 291

APPENDIX II
TABLE 1, A

Chart of Major Variables, Means and Variances, Collegians and Seminarians

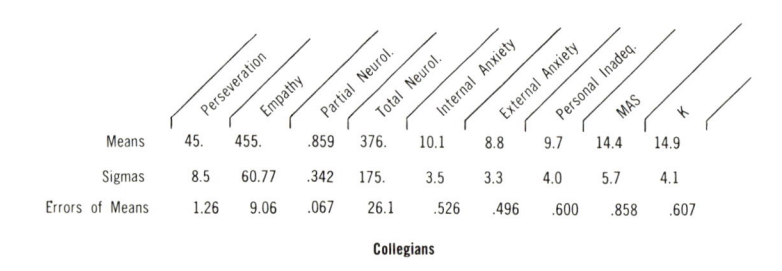

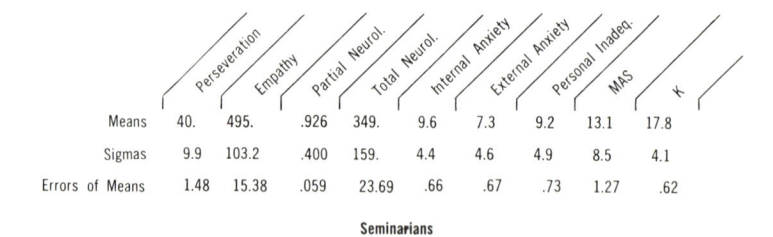

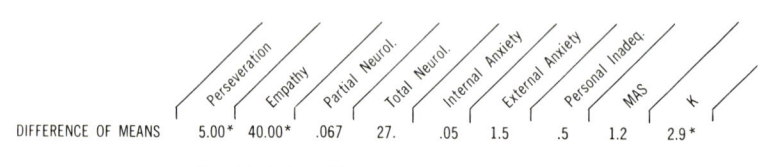

	Perseveration	Empathy	Partial Neurol.	Total Neurol.	Internal Anxiety	External Anxiety	Personal Inadeq.	MAS	K
Means	45.	455.	.859	376.	10.1	8.8	9.7	14.4	14.9
Sigmas	8.5	60.77	.342	175.	3.5	3.3	4.0	5.7	4.1
Errors of Means	1.26	9.06	.067	26.1	.526	.496	.600	.858	.607

Collegians

	Perseveration	Empathy	Partial Neurol.	Total Neurol.	Internal Anxiety	External Anxiety	Personal Inadeq.	MAS	K
Means	40.	495.	.926	349.	9.6	7.3	9.2	13.1	17.8
Sigmas	9.9	103.2	.400	159.	4.4	4.6	4.9	8.5	4.1
Errors of Means	1.48	15.38	.059	23.69	.66	.67	.73	1.27	.62

Seminarians

	Perseveration	Empathy	Partial Neurol.	Total Neurol.	Internal Anxiety	External Anxiety	Personal Inadeq.	MAS	K
DIFFERENCE OF MEANS	5.00*	40.00*	.067	27.	.05	1.5	.5	1.2	2.9*

* Significant at the .01 level.

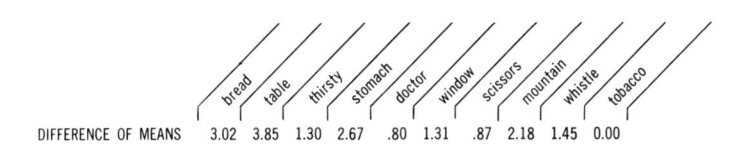

APPENDIX II
TABLE 1, B

Chart of Ten Critical Words on LLS
Means and Variances: Collegians and Seminarians

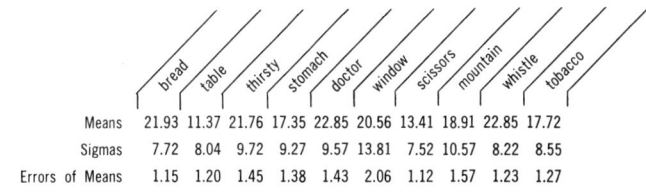

	bread	table	thirsty	stomach	doctor	window	scissors	mountain	whistle	tobacco
Means	21.93	11.37	21.76	17.35	22.85	20.56	13.41	18.91	22.85	17.72
Sigmas	7.72	8.04	9.72	9.27	9.57	13.81	7.52	10.57	8.22	8.55
Errors of Means	1.15	1.20	1.45	1.38	1.43	2.06	1.12	1.57	1.23	1.27

Collegians

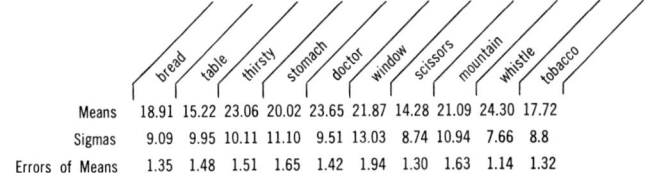

	bread	table	thirsty	stomach	doctor	window	scissors	mountain	whistle	tobacco
Means	18.91	15.22	23.06	20.02	23.65	21.87	14.28	21.09	24.30	17.72
Sigmas	9.09	9.95	10.11	11.10	9.51	13.03	8.74	10.94	7.66	8.8
Errors of Means	1.35	1.48	1.51	1.65	1.42	1.94	1.30	1.63	1.14	1.32

Seminarians

	bread	table	thirsty	stomach	doctor	window	scissors	mountain	whistle	tobacco
DIFFERENCE OF MEANS	3.02	3.85	1.30	2.67	.80	1.31	.87	2.18	1.45	0.00

APPENDIX II
TABLE 1, C

Chart of Five Words Used Both in Pre-Threat EDR Measure And in EDR Measure After Threatening Essay

	Non Threat					After Threat				
	word 1	word 2	word 3	word 4	word 5	word 1	word 2	word 3	word 4	word 5
Means	523.63	360.07	480.41	405.02	348.13	310.13	222.72	298.72	356.20	266.87
Sigmas	296.85	238.91	208.62	277.85	252.89	261.31	214.30	250.67	237.19	202.35
Errors of Means	44.24	35.61	31.09	41.41	37.69	38.94	31.94	37.36	35.35	30.15
Differences in words before and after, all less after	213.50	137.35	181.69	48.82*	81.26*					

Collegians

	Non Threat					After Threat				
	word 1	word 2	word 3	word 4	word 5	word 1	word 2	word 3	word 4	word 5
Means	492.00	311.91	457.33	402.43	331.30	295.57	241.07	297.33	295.91	234.74
Sigmas	250.43	206.60	195.85	220.84	236.96	209.00	209.59	197.23	191.21	205.61
Errors of Means	37.32	30.79	29.19	32.91	35.31	31.15	31.23	29.39	28.50	30.64
Differences in words before and after, all less after	196.43	70.84*	160.00	106.52	93.56					

Seminarians

| DIFFERENCE OF MEANS | 31.63 | 48.16 | 23.08 | 2.59 | 16.83 | 14.56 | 18.35 | 1.39 | 60.29 | 29.13 |

* Not significant @ .05, by formula for correlated means.

APPENDIX III
FIGURE 1

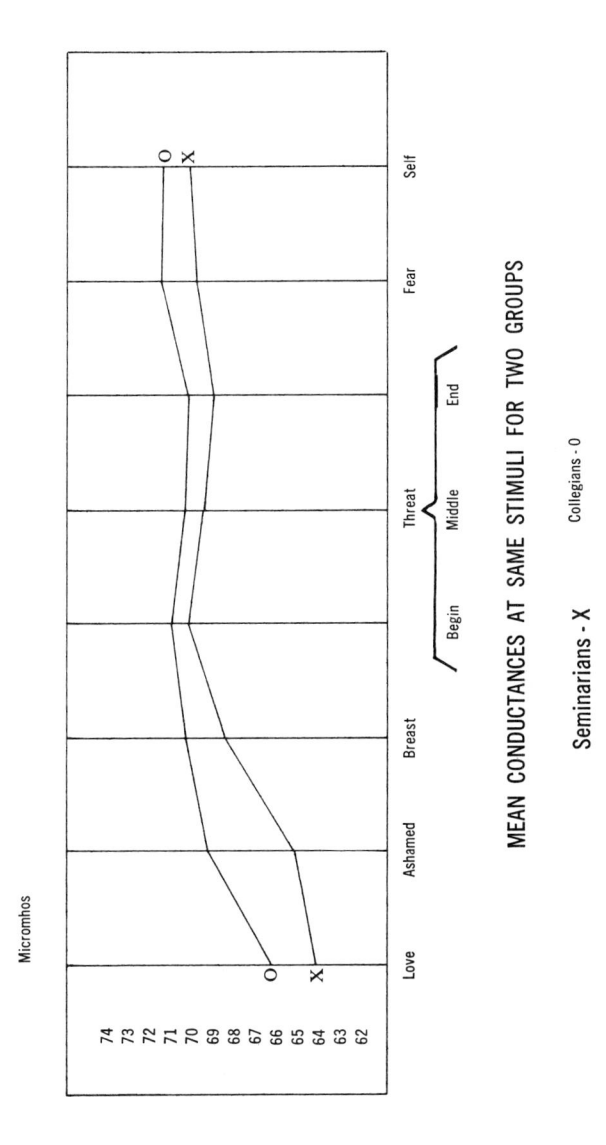

MEAN CONDUCTANCES AT SAME STIMULI FOR TWO GROUPS

Seminarians - X   Collegians - O

124 PERSONALITY OF SEMINARIANS

APPENDIX III
FIGURE 2

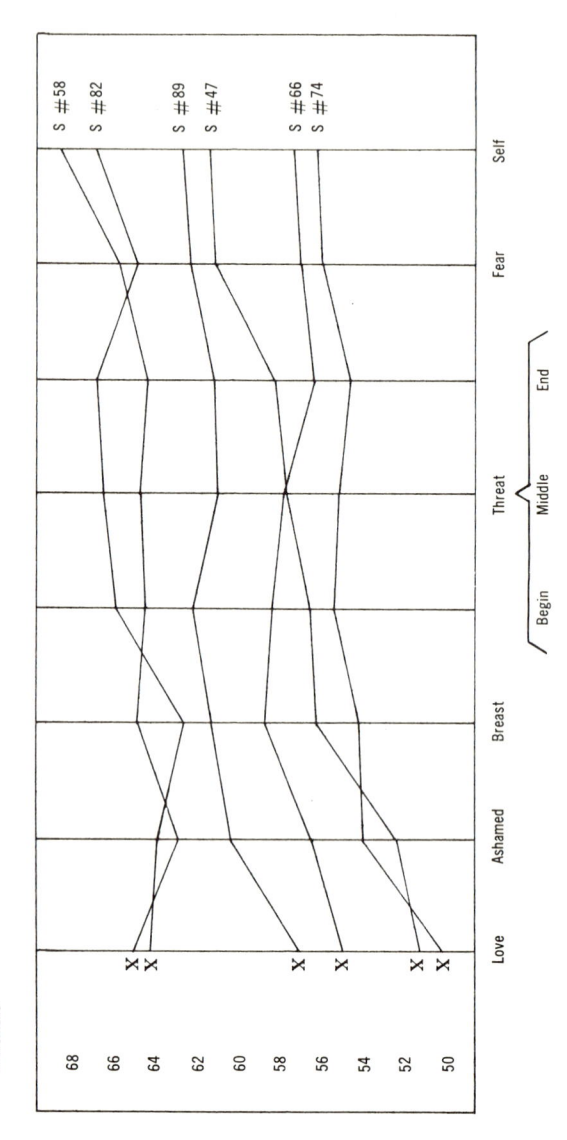

SINGLE SUBJECTS' CONDUCTANCES AT SAME STIMULI FOR SEMINARIANS

Seminarians - X

APPENDIX III
FIGURE 3

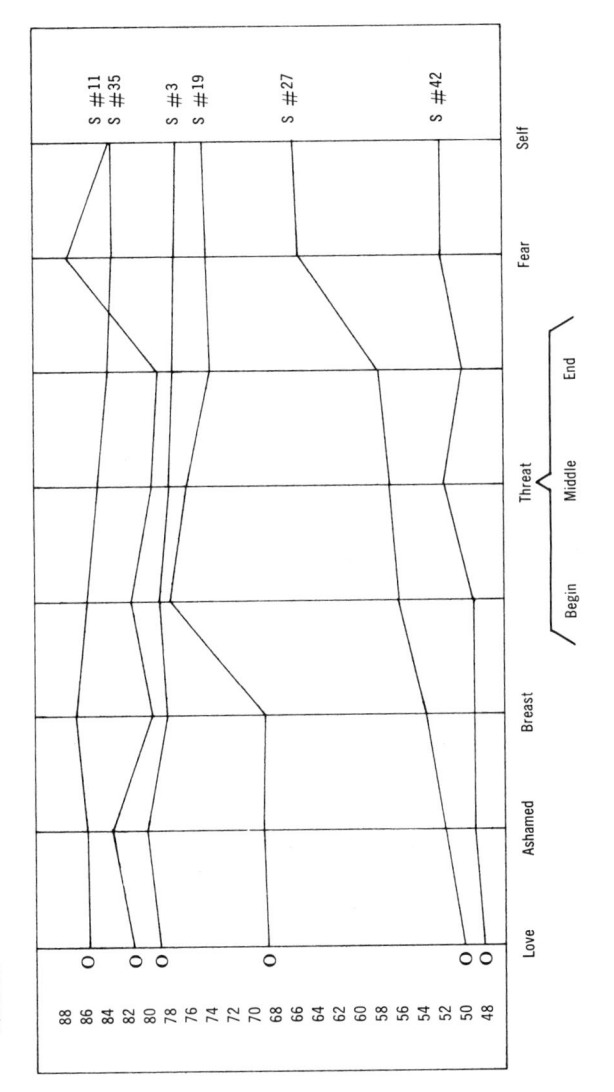

SINGLE SUBJECTS' CONDUCTANCES AT SAME STIMULI FOR COLLEGIANS

Collegians - 0

APPENDIX IV
THE RICE-LE SENNE-BERGER SCALE*
(Regarding interpretation, see end of Appendices)

Use an IBM answer sheet with spaces for five choices and 64 questions; use soft lead pencils; be sure answers correspond to numbers on questions; work briskly and answer all questions; first choices are always best.

In regard to your activities and movements are you:
1. a. lively and active (with natural urge to action)
   b. or ordinarily calm and poised?
2. a. always devoted to your duty of state of life (the work you have to do)
   b. or only from time to time
   c. or generally lazy?
3. a. ordinarily occupied (even during leisure moments)
   b. or tending to take it easy?
4. a. inclined to be negligent in appointed tasks (preferring those of your own choice)
   b. or not?
5. a. negligent in doing occasional duties (such as letter-writing, business affairs, writing a paper, studying, etc.?)
   b. or diligent about carrying out immediately these same duties?
6. a. inclined to give up your plans easily whenever you meet with obstacles
   b. or persevering (stimulated by obstacles)
   c. or entirely obstinate (stubborn, won't accept a word of advice)?
7. a. impulsive (making decisions without reflecting)
   b. or circumspect (reflecting, examining the affair)
   c. or a man of principles (acting according to established principles)?

---

* Patrick Rice, S.J., revised the English sentence structure of the whole test.

8. a. decided in difficult cases (usually making a rapid decision)
   b. or undecided (hesitant)

In regard to your sentiments and feelings, are you:
9. a. violent in your speech (warming up, exaggerating, raising your voice, etc.?)
   b. or cold and objective (saying things calmly?)
10. a. susceptible or inclined to being in bad humor
    b. or gentle, meek, even-tempered?
11. a. gay and lively, pleased with life
    b. or melancholic and sad
    c. or always calm and in good humor
    d. or alternately gay and sad?
12. a. anxious and disturbed about the future
    b. or not (feeling that everything will be all right?)

In your rather permanent dispositions, are you:
13. a. easily consoled after losing cherished friends
    b. or impressed by the loss for a long time?
14. a. immediately reconciled (after being impatient or even angry)
    b. or in bad humor for a little while
    c. or difficult to reconcile?
15. a. inconstant in your friendships, your sympathies (abandoning your friends, turning against them)
    b. or constant?
16. a. attached to things of the past (friends of childhood days, your home, etc.)
    b. or interested in innovations (new impressions, new friends, etc.)?
17. a. persistent in your opinions
    b. or easily influenced by new ideas?
18. a. prone to like changes (in regulations, in furniture)
    b. or a person of fixed habits?

19. a. often concerned with great projects, but without realizing them
    b. or not?
20. a. guided in your actions by the distant future
    b. or by the thought of immediate results?
21. a. generally faithful to acting on principles
    b. or often in contradiction to them?

In your thinking and reasoning, are you
22. a. of quick understanding (grasping new ideas without difficulty)
    b. or not?
23. a. of keen intelligence (understanding clearly and being able to explain to others)
    b. or of superficial intelligence (judging according to passing impressions and hence contradicting yourself)?
24. a. practical, with common sense (knowing how to make the most of what you have)
    b. or without practical judgment?
25. a. autonomous in your opinions
    b. or inclined to repeat the opinions of others?
26. a. inclined to intervene in all questions with a decisive opinion
    b. or not?
27. a. talented in mathematics
    b. or in languages
    c. or in music
    d. or in art
    e. or acting (theatrical talent)?
28. a. quick-witted (finding witty answers easily)
    b. or not?
29. a. an agreeable conversationalist
    b. or inclined to take the lead in conversation, to monopolize it
    c. or silent and introverted?
30. a. confused and diffuse in your narrations

b. or concise and direct?
31. a. able to speak in public without preparation (able to improvise)
    b. or not?
32. a. a good observer (noticing details where other people neglect them)
    b. or not (unable to see objects or details right before your eyes)?
33. a. gifted with a very good ear for music?
    b. or a good one?
    c. or a poor one?
34. a. skillful (at various types of work)
    b. or awkward (not knowing how to begin or to go about things)?

In your habitual inclinations, are you
35. a. greatly concerned about eating and drinking well (preoccupied and disturbed about it)
    b. or not?
36. a. satisfied with yourself (thinking you do better than others)
    b. or dissatisfied (always criticizing yourself)
    c. or neither the one nor the other?
37. a. vain (liking to look at yourself in the mirror)
    b. or little disturbed about your appearance?
38. a. ambitious (for consideration, honors, distinction, first place)
    b. or indifferent to these considerations?
39. a. miserly (collecting for the sake of collecting)
    b. or thrifty (storing for the future)
    c. or wasteful (of money, clothes, paper, light)?
40. a. authoritative (wanting to boss everywhere, never giving in)
    b. or inclined to let each one have his way?
41. a. compassionate, and usually willing to help men and animals

b. or not (selfish before others' suffering)
c. or cruel (taking pleasure in seeing others suffer)?
42. a. very patriotic (proud of your nationality, sensitive to criticism of it)
b. or not?
43. a. perfectly at ease, natural, whenever you have to meet with new company
c. or affected, unnatural in words and actions (giving yourself airs, playing a part)?
44. a. demonstrative (expressing your ideas and likes, vehemently defending them)
b. or closed-up, taciturn (keeping everything to yourself)
45. a. inclined to execute your projects honorably (straightforward)
b. or with diplomacy, hiding your real intentions (though without intrigue)?
46. a. perfectly truthful in your conversation
b. or inclined to exaggerate
c. or to add, to embellish
d. or to lie?
47. a. friendly with children (willing to play with them, liked by them)
b. or not?
48. a. courageous (attracted by danger, fire, riot, outbreak, accidents, etc.)
b. or pusillanimous (evading danger as much as possible)
49. a. attracted by activities away from home (clubs, meetings, concerts, theatre)
b. or happy to recreate yourself with the family
c. or inclined to withdraw from society (to be solitary)?
50. a. inclined to talk about objects, things
b. or about people?
51. a. inclined to talk about yourself
b. or not?
52. a. a great reader
b. or do you read little?
53. a. able to relate precisely and in an orderly manner what

you have read
- b. or in a confused and disorderly way?
54. a. inclined to dwell on abstract subjects (philosophy, religion, etc.)
    b. or not?
55. a. a passionate collector (of antiques, plants, insects, stamps, post-cards, etc.)
    b. or not?
56. a. readily drawn to become enthusiastic about new theories (vegetarianism, sight without glasses, simplified spelling, etc.)
    b. or not?
57. a. a lover of sports (baseball, hockey, hunting, fishing, etc.)
    b. or not?
58. a. a lover of intellectual games (checkers, chess, bridge, crossword puzzles)
    b. or not?
59. a. a lover of games of chance (roulette, bingo, dice, etc.)
    b. or not?
60. a. absent-minded (inattentive, a dreamer)
    b. or on the alert (always attentive to the action or task of the present moment)?
61. a. neat and orderly (with regard to clothes, room, regular penmanship)
    b. or disorderly (with everything hanging and lying around)?
62. a. punctual (on time everywhere, doing the prescribed task on time)
    b. or not?
63. a. inclined to talk loudly (in a strident voice)
    b. or in an even, calm, poised tone of voice
    c. or in a strong, joyful voice, with rising inflections
    d. or in a biting and dry voice?
64. a. inclined to laugh a great deal
    b. or little
    c. or never?

APPENDIX V
WEISGERBER — PERSEVERATION
(Regarding interpretation, see end of Appendices)

Use IBM answer sheet with five columns and over 50 questions. Use soft lead pencils and blacken the spaces in the columns which correspond to your choices; be sure numbers on questions correspond to those on answer sheets; work briskly; if the columns have letters on top; replace them with numbers, 0 through 4. If you elect option 3 for question 1 blacken the space in third column after question 1. Be sure to read each question carefully, and be frank and earnest, that is, if a certain choice seems to fit you or nearly so, make the proper mark. You do not know at this point whether a certain answer is damaging or otherwise, so be truthful, as far as you can. Do not skip any question. Best choices are the first to come to mind.

1. When you are working on some task, or trying to solve a problem, do you find it hard to lay it aside for interruptions? (This does not mean a personal problem or one that is a source of worry.)
   2) occasionally, 1) seldom, 4) almost always, 0) never, 3) often.
2. If you have laid aside a task of this kind, do you find that it still keeps coming back to your mind?
   4) almost always, 3) often, 2) occasionally, 0) never, 1) seldom.
3. After a trip by boat, train, car, or other vehicle, do you seem to keep on hearing the noise or feeling the motion for a time?
   1) seldom, 0) never, 4) almost always, 2) occasionally, 3) often.
4. Do these sensations later come back in your dreams?
   2) occasionally, 1) seldom, 3) often, 4) almost always, 0) never.
5. Does it usually annoy you to have many different tasks or duties to look after?
   3) much, 0) not at all, 2) somewhat, 1) a little bit, 4) so much that I worry and get anxious.

6. Do you dream at night?
   0) never, 4) nearly every night, 1) not more than 5 or 6 times a year, 3) about once or twice a week, 2) about once a month.
7. Do you dream about things that have recently happened?
   4) practically whenever I dream, 1) seldom, 2) occasionally, 0) never, 3) often.
8. Do tunes keep running through your mind without the least effort or intention on your part?
   3) often, 2) occasionally, 4) constantly, 0) never, 1) seldom.
9. When unexpectedly addressed or asked a question which you know well enough, but have not been thinking about at the time, can you answer easily and quickly?
   0) practically always, 4) practically never, 3) not quite half the time, 2) more than half the time, 1) usually.
10. Do you like changes in the routine of life?
    2) like routine in regard to certain things only, 1) like a little routine but the less the better, 3) like routine for most of my day with some room for variety, 4) any change is a nuisance, 0) prefer no routine whatsoever.
11. When you become angry, do you get over it fairly quickly?
    3) seldom, 2) occasionally, 0) almost always, 4) never, 1) often.
12. Do you worry about things?
    1) seldom, 0) hardly at all, 2) occasionally, 3) often, 4) extremely often.
13. If you have some worry, does it keep coming back to mind when you don't want to think of it (if you have no worries, check "never")?
    1) seldom, 3) often, 0) never, 4) constantly, 2) occasionally.
14. When you turn back to a task after a brief interruption, can you get the task back into mind readily, so that the former thoughts come back easily? (i.e. you feel you "have your bearings" at once.)
    2) usually, 4) very seldom, 1) about 9 times out of 10, 3) about half the time, 0) always.

15. Do you get over a disappointment very quickly?
    2) occasionally, 0) practically always, 1) often, 3) seldom, 4) never.
16. Do you dream about things that worry you (if you have no worries, check "never")?
    4) constantly, 2) occasionally, 1) seldom, 0) never, 3) often.
17. When you have seen a very tragic play or movie, does the emotion linger with you for hours afterwards?
    3) often, 0) never, 2) occasionally, 4) practically always, 1) seldom.
18. Do lines of poetry, words, or phrases spontaneously keep coming to your mind?
    1) seldom, 0) never, 3) often, 2) occasionally, 4) constantly.
19. After you have lived in one room or place for some time, do you find it hard to settle down to work in new quarters?
    0) not at all, 4) extremely hard, 2) a bit hard, 3) noticeably hard, 1) not worth mentioning.
20. If a little thing goes wrong early in the day, does it put you in a bad mood?
    3) often, 1) seldom, 4) practically always, 0) never, 2) occasionally.
21. When you have an important or somewhat unfamiliar task ahead of you and the day for it approaches, do you catch yourself thinking about it even when you don't want to?
    4) extremely often, 2) occasionally, 0) never, 1) seldom, 3) often.
22. Are you aware of being bothered by unimportant or useless thoughts or ideas that keep coming back to your mind?
    3) often, 2) occasionally, 0) never, 1) seldom, 4) extremely often.
23. Do you find it hard to shake off a spell of the blues?
    2) occasionally, 1) seldom, 4) extremely often, 3) often, 0) never.
24. Are you generally able to keep your mind on a task or job?
    3) easily, 1) with great difficulty, 4) quickly become absorbed in it, 0) yes, but with great difficulty, 2) with moderate difficulty.

25. When you awaken during a dream, does it continue when you are asleep again?
    4) almost always, 2) occasionally, 0) never, 1) seldom, 3) often.
26. When you cannot recall a name, does it disturb you until you can recall it?
    4) almost always, 0) never, 3) often, 1) seldom, 2) occasionally.
27. Can you change from one activity to another readily?
    3) seldom, 4) never, 2) often, 1) occasionally, 0) practically always.
28. When you are asked a question you cannot answer, does it bother you afterwards until you have the answer?
    2) occasionally, 3) often, 0) never, 4) practically always, 1) seldom.
29. Do you ever carry out an activity somewhat automatically, having temporarily forgotten the purpose of the act?
    4) extremely often, 3) often, 1) seldom, 2) occasionally, 0) never.
30. Do you fall easily into a steady routine without giving it any particular thought or effort (e.g. doing the same things at the same time day after day)?
    2) occasionally, 0) never, 4) practically always, 1) seldom, 3) often.
31. Do you like to dwell on ideas, turning them over and over in your mind and examining them from all angles?
    3) often, 1) seldom, 2) occasionally, 0) never, 4) constantly.
32. Do you prefer to stick to a task until it is finished, rather than do just part of it at a time?
    2) occasionally, 3) often, 1) seldom, 0) never, 4) practically always.
33. When you are reading something interesting, do you find it hard to lay it aside for a while?
    0) never, 4) practically aways, 1) seldom, 3) often, 2) occasionally.
34. When you plan something, do your plans keep coming back to mind, even though they are complete and you are

not afraid you have overlooked something?
1) seldom, 4) practically always, 0) never, 3) often, 2) occasionally.
35. In conversation, do you find that one thing leads to another and you tend to get off on some other subject?
4) never, 3) seldom, 1) often, 2) occasionally, 0) extremely often.
36. Do you do better by thinking straight through a problem from start to finish, rather than by frequently dropping it so as to take it up again later?
3) often, 1) seldom, 0) never, 2) occasionally, 4) invariably.
37. When you are in a very good mood and things seem rosy, do you tend to stay that way for some time, despite *minor* difficulties and troubles?
0) I change for no apparent reason, 3) serious matters upset me, 4) nothing can upset me, 1) trivial things upset me, 2) minor difficulties upset me.
38. Do you day dream?
2) occasionally, 0) never, 4) extremely often, 1) seldom, 3) often.
39. Do you prefer to do one task at a time and finish it before going on to another, rather than to have several "irons in the fire" at the same time?
4) cannot stand more than one at a time, 1) slightly prefer, 0) do not at all prefer, 2) somewhat prefer, 3) much prefer.
40. Do you find that you seem to pick up the latest slang at once and automatically, without particularly wishing to do so?
4) practically always, 2) occasionally, 3) often, 0) never, 1) seldom.

APPENDIX VI

COMMENTS UPON THE EGO-INVOLVING INSTRUCTIONS

1. For the Collegians:
These suggested the following threats: that perhaps the

student does not really know who his parents are; or whether he is an orphan or not; or whether he is circumcised or not; and that if he is not, then he cannot have the full pleasures of marital intercourse; that the science of medicine is now doing something about these things.

2. For the Seminarians:
These suggest the following threats: that perhaps the reason for the changed conditions regarding celibacy of the clergy are partly the moral lapses in the past; that clergy in general are insincere and full of pretence; that the black garments are only a cover to hide their ambiguity and insincerity; that the clergy of many faiths, upon dialogue and discussion, are coming to realize these facts and are trying to do something about them. (Needless to say, the two essays had been matched to each other with respect to their physiological effects.)

APPENDIX VII

THE EXISTENTIAL STUDY BY F. C. THORNE

Limited Circulation

1. T F It is hard for me to get out of bed in the morning.
2. T F I feel bored a lot of the time.
3. T F Up to now, I have not been too successful in life.
4. T F Nothing exciting ever seems to happen to me.
5. T F In general, I like myself.
6. T F I have never found a kind of work which really interested me.
7. T F As I grow older, I seem to have fewer real friends.
8. T F I daydream often about being a very successful person.
9. T F I don't like to stay very long in any one place.
10. T F I haven't ever been really successful at anything.
11. T F Sometimes I feel ashamed over my lack of achievement.

12. T F I feel that I am just as good as anybody else.
13. T F I have never been able to actualize my potentialities.
14. T F Life is very exciting and I wouldn't miss a minute of it.
15. T F I have just about had it as far as experiencing any more troubles in life.
16. T F Life no longer has much meaning for me.
17. T F Nobody would have much of a chance against an atom bomb.
18. T F It makes me nervous if people look at me.
19. T F I have always been very popular with other people.
20. T F I have always been embarrassed over my looks.
21. T F I never had any trouble getting along with the opposite sex.
22. T F Most people seem to like me very well.
23. T F I feel that I am a real person.
24. T F I don't feel as intelligent as other people.
25. T F My sympathy is with the underdog.
26. T F I feel guilty because of the mistakes I have made in life.
27. T F I would do things differently if I could live my life over.
28. T F I have had a good life.
29. T F I don't have much hope for the future.
30. T F One of my worst fears is of having a mental breakdown.
31. T F I was always considered to be a frail child.
32. T F I like most other people.
33. T F I never have much trouble making friends.
34. T F Sometimes I have feared I might crack up mentally.
35. T F I don't understand the meanings of life.
36. T F I often get tired of my job.
37. T F I have had periods of confusion where I didn't know what I was doing.
38. T F I am more than "breaking even" in life.
39. T F It is hard to find something interesting to do.
40. T F I can't stand to be alone for very long.

41. T F I consider myself a rather uninteresting person.
42. T F I often thank the Lord for my blessings.
43. T F I don't have much confidence in myself.
44. T F I get too excited over little things in life.
45. T F Making mistakes bothers me too much.
46. T F Inwardly, I don't feel that I am a strong person.
47. T F It's best not to be too familiar with strangers.
48. T F I hope to go to Heaven.
49. T F I often pray for strength to face life.
50. T F Something is missing in my life.
51. T F I often wish that I were a child again.
52. T F I have lost my respect for most people.
53. T F Most people have treated me fairly enough in life.
54. T F Sometimes I feel that I am a misfit.
55. T F As a child, I felt lonely most of the time.
56. T F I don't really feel at home anywhere.
57. T F The world is not a very friendly place.
58. T F Life seems to be passing me by.
59. T F All in all, I am satisfied with my life.
60. T F I often have trouble finding something interesting to do.
61. T F My life is pretty empty.
62. T F I consider myself a successful person.
63. T F I am a rather lonely person.
64. T F Time passes too fast to suit me.
65. T F Somehow, I have never seemed to "find" myself.
66. T F The greatest trouble is Man's inhumanity to man.
67. T F Nothing exciting seems to happen any more.
68. T F Some of the highest moments of my life have come from music and art.
69. T F My greatest gratification is helping other people.
70. T F My greatest need is to be a real person.
71. T F I like to excel in whatever I do.
72. T F Often I just don't know what to do with myself.
73. T F I don't like my personality.
74. T F I have never been really close to anybody in my life.
75. T F I am getting deeper into debt all the time.

76. T F I am always behind in my work.
77. T F I have trouble budgeting my money.
78. T F I have a savings bank account.
79. T F I have trouble meeting the installment plan payments.
80. T F I wish I had more real friends.
81. T F I don't make friends easily.
82. T F I like to be corrected when I make a mistake.
83. T F I am afraid of ending up in a hospital or institution.
84. T F It wouldn't embarrass me to go on relief.
85. T F I have enough saved up to take care of me in old age.
86. T F I have a lot of vague feelings of insecurity.
87. T F I have won a lot of honors in my life.
88. T F I consider myself just as good as anybody else.
89. T F I would like to see a psychiatrist.
90. T F I am happiest when I'm working.
91. T F Passing leisure time is hard for me.
92. T F I have a lot of hobbies.
93. T F I always try to carry my share of the load.
94. T F Life has dealt me a lot of dirty deals.
95. T F I have a lot of vague fears and anxieties.
96. T F I don't have a care in the world.
97. T F I belong to a lot of clubs and organizations.
98. T F The rest of the world is leaving me behind.
99. T F I am always trying to improve myself.
100. T F It has bothered me to answer these questions.

APPENDIX VIII

SOCIAL STATUS STUDY, BY F. C. THORNE

Limited Circulation

1. T F I would like to serve as chairman of public meetings.
2. T F It bothers me not to be invited when a friend has a party.
3. T F Social standing is very important to me.

4. T F The members of my family have always gotten along well.
5. T F When I was in school, I was captain of a team.
6. T F I try to vote in all elections.
7. T F I go to parties at least once a week.
8. T F I don't try to keep up with the Joneses.
9. T F Family life has always meant a lot to me.
10. T F I would rather take orders than give them.
11. T F I try to keep up with public affairs.
12. T F Small talk at parties is easy for me.
13. T F I am proud of my family background.
14. T F It is important to know the right people.
15. T F Other people look up to me as a leader.
16. T F I always contribute to charity fund raising drives.
17. T F I like to go bowling or other places with a crowd.
18. T F It is important for me to have good clothes.
19. T F When I was a child, our family did a lot of things together.
20. T F I would like to be a member of an athletic team.
21. T F I like to do volunteer work for public organizations.
22. T F I spend a lot of time alone doing things by myself.
23. T F I would rather have a foreign car than an American model.
24. T F It is not good for husband and wife both to work.
25. T F I don't like to take orders from anybody.
26. T F I would like to be called for jury duty.
27. T F I would like to live way out in the country away from people.
28. T F I never like to have dates with a homely person.
29. T F If I had a mentally defective child, I would try to raise it at home.
30. T F Taking part in politics interests me.
31. T F I have given blood at a blood bank drawing.
32. T F I try to go out of my way to be friendly with strangers.
33. T F I like to take part in high society events.

34. T F The members of a family should always stick together.
35. T F I am too shy to speak up in public meetings.
36. T F If I saw a person being attacked by a thug, I would try to take their part.
37. T F I have belonged to a lot of clubs and groups in my life.
38. T F I would like to own a Cadillac or a Lincoln.
39. T F I wouldn't care if I never saw some of my relatives again.
40. T F I wouldn't take the Presidency if you offered it to me.
41. T F I would like to join the Peace Corps.
42. T F I like to have a lot of people around all the time.
43. T F People of distinction interest me.
44. T F Old people are better off by themselves.
45. T F When I was in school, I was something of a wallflower.
46. T F It is best to mind your own business and not get into trouble if you see somebody else doing wrong.
47. T F I am a member of at least one fraternal organization.
48. T F I would travel a long way to see a famous person.
49. T F If one member of the family gets into financial trouble the others should get together and bail him out.
50. T F If there is another war, I hope I don't get drafted.
51. T F I am dissatisfied with the way my State government is doing things.
52. T F I prefer small parties rather than large crowds.
53. T F I like to go with upper class people.
54. T F I wouldn't want to live with my in-laws.
55. T F I would rather watch sports than take part in them.
56. T F I approve of spending money to explore outer space.
57. T F I wish I had more friends.
58. T F I want my children to get into a higher social class.
59. T F The State should take care of cripples and incurable cases.

60. T F I would like to learn more about Civil Defense.
61. T F I approve of the way the Federal government is handling things.
62. T F I like to attend cocktail parties.
63. T F Whatever I have, I want it to be of the best.
64. T F Parents should keep a tight control over their children.
65. T F The country should lead the way in making the world free for Democracy.
66. T F I always believe in telling people what I think at public meetings.
67. T F I do a lot of entertaining.
68. T F I live in one of the better parts of town (country).
69. T F Children should be allowed to drive cars as soon as they are old enough to get a license.
70. T F I enjoy dangerous sports.
71. T F Every young person should contribute part of his time to try to improve conditions in the world.
72. T F I have spent a lot of time drinking in bars and grills.
73. T F I like to trade in smart shops.
74. T F I would really worry if one of my children dropped out of college.
75. T F I would like to be an astronaut and take a flight in space.
76. T F I try to do a good turn every day.
77. T F If I went to Europe, I would rather go with a guided tour.
78. T F When I travel, I would like to stay at all the best places.
79. T F Praise rather than punishment should be used to control children.
80. T F It makes me nervous to be the center of attention.
81. T F It is wrong to throw trash on the highways.
82. T F I seem to get along better with older people.
83. T F People have called me snobbish.
84. T F Parents should be very strict with children.
85. T F I daydream a lot of being a great leader.

86. T F I take an interest in civic affairs by working for community organization.
87. T F Most of my friends seem to be younger than I am.
88. T F I couldn't care less what other people think of me.
89. T F I believe that sparing the rod spoils the child.
90. T F I don't like to be the first to try something new.
91. T F I never break the law if I can help it.
92. T F I like to go on picnics.
93. T F Someday I would like to have a big yacht.
94. T F I like to play games with children.
95. T F I never take a chance if I can help it.
96. T F I try to give money to every worthwhile charity.
97. T F I prefer solitary sports like hunting and fishing.
98. T F I can't stand social climbers.
99. T F I believe in having big families.
100. T F Pain doesn't bother me.

SUPPLEMENT TO THE TESTS

1. The Thorne (revised) test is a self-audit and social scale. It yields a score for "self worth" as well as one for "social personality," as estimated by the self. It is as yet only in the experimental stages. Its authors, F. C. Thorne and co-workers, are preparing national norms. Permission to quote this material was granted by Dr. Thorne who is the editor of the *Journal of Clinical Psychology*, Brandon, Vermont.

2. The Weisgerber perseveration scale has been duly described in our text. It also yields two factors, the one an emotional one, and the other sensory-rational. The citations in our text refer to these factors.

3. The Rice-LeSenne-Berger is a character test, yielding three factors, one for emotionality, one for action tendency, and one for perseveration.

Any one wishing to use these tests must by all means get in contact with the author of this book or one of his assistants.

GLOSSARY

Adjustment (Adjust) — A quality whereby a person habitually suits his actions to the needs of the situation, whether these be the biological or the psychological. Biological adjustment is usually designated as adaptation. It should be noted here that every "actual" adjustment involves a change in the thing which is adjusted. This change may be radical, (deeply seated in the organism); as in changing from one society to another; or only minor, as in changing one's style of dress to become in style.

Analysis of Variance — A technique for manipulating scores, obtained from a large number of groups, so as to be able to tell from what sources the differences in averages for the several groups might have arisen; that is to say, are the differences due, mostly, to heterogeneity within each of the several groups, or not? May they possibly be due to differences in the manner of treatment of the several groups, while collecting the scores, etc., etc.?

Anxiety — Fear without an object. Countless authors have tried to show what it is that really makes a person anxious. No common opinion is known to the author at this time. However, it would be safe to say that in anxiety the subject says he does not know the cause, whereas in fear he thinks he does know. Walker and Nicolay, in their fourfold classification of modes of anxiety, merely give the results of mathematical treatment of scores (factor analysis) and their classification is not to be taken as one based upon the data of internal experience on the part of the person who takes their test (the modified Taylor Anxiety Scale).

Aptitude — A special propensity to excel in one trait, which has been manifest over the years. It resembles habit except that it is more specific in its mode of reference, and more modern in terminology. Examples: musical aptitude; habit of smoking.

Attitude — A mental habit or set whereby there is, in a person, a readiness to perform along a given line, prior to the actual occurrence of the stimulus for any reaction whatever. Example: Racial attitude toward Mongols or Arabs, on the part of Chinese or Slavs.

Character — Life dominated by principles. Note especially, the principles may, in a particular case, actually be false in themselves or even morally bad, but the response to them is given, more or less automatically. Example: The determination to kill anyone who is not of one's own religion. It may also be vaguely conscious or even almost totally unconscious. Example: to make the sign of the cross in every dangerous or threatening situation.

Conductance change — The reciprocal of the resistance change. Example: if 10,000 ohms minus 9,000 ohms is a resistance change, then 1/10,000 ohms minus 1/9,000 ohms is its corresponding conductance change. Logarithms of both these quantities will facilitate the process.

Correlation — A technical term used to designate the "going-togetherness" of two or more qualities or traits. If this is positive, then the higher the one trait, the higher the other; if it is negative, the higher the one, the lower the other. Example of the first: intelligence correlated with grades in college. Example of the second, fearfulness and anxiety correlate negatively with goodness or achievement. The usual figure for correlation is in percentages or decimals. Thus a correlation of .45 between two variables means that there is about 20% communality between the factors responsible for the one and those responsible for the other. In still simpler terms, if the correlation between intelligence and college grades in a particular group is .45, then about 20% of the factors which are responsible for college grades are traceable to the native intelligence of the students.

Ego — Traditionally (before Freud) taken to mean the self, as subject of all its actions and attributes, whether known or not, conscious or not, correctly judged or not. Ego, ever since James has been either directly known by reflection (the scholastic perfect reflection), or indirectly implied in the fact that "I know I act as if all my acts are mine and those of no one else."

Electrodermal Response — This was formerly known as Galvanic Skin Response (GSR). The momentary rise in skin conductivity (drop in resistance) following shortly after any one of countless stresses in life, or predicaments in life; in these the organism finds itself more or less sensitive to the various conditions. It is found to be the most sensitive of all the physical indicators of **transitory** emotional response.

Emotion — A disturbed condition or state of the organism, resulting from an external or an internal stimulation. It thus has both mental and physiological concomitants. It is either a long-enduring state, or a momentary reaction. As a state, it is related to the temperament of a person and has been described in numerous different terms and categories. As a momentary disturbance, its bodily accompaniments are easily measured. They are mainly: 1) changes in breathing; 2) in blood pressure; 3) in pulse; and 4) in heart condition. The estimates of these changes, which accompany each and every emotional outburst, contribute to the science of lie-detection. The more precise and accurate determination of these changes, especially as they are related to long-term emotionality, constitute the science of personality assessment as used in this book.

Empathy — A feeling with and in another person. The one seems to identify with the other, and to re-experience the same feelings as the other. This must not be confused with **sympathy**, which is a kind of pity, had by one person, at the thought of his being NOT so bad off as the other. Both terms are being studied in the process of personality assessment, but the term "empathy" is much more common today and there are several well validated paper-and-pencil tests for this trait, of which the Loyola Language Study is only one.

Gestalt — A movement in Germany and Austria, counteracting the views of sensists and associationists. The theory holds that there are involved in every act of sensory perception: a. The present stimulation; b. the past experience of the person who is viewing the present object; and c. the present state and mental attitudes of the observer.

Haggard Transformation — A modification of the Ohms Resistance score for EDR (GSR) in order to: a. normalize the distribution; b. to make each score independent of the basic resistance at the time; and c. to make the units equal throughout the whole range of scores from high to low.

Intelligence — The capacity to do abstract thinking, to understand relations, and to reason about the future consequences of one's acts (Binet). Wechsler, a prominent intelligence tester, includes in this notion that capacity to react globally to the many aspects of a given situation, whether this be loaded with emotion or not. The commonest acceptable definition for adults seems to be that of Binet.

Mental Illness — A state of the person, in which the mental faculties are not functioning up to their expected level; the person is therefore somehow or other not capable of functioning effectively in the ordinary life situations.

MMPI — Minnesota Multiphasic Personality Inventory

Neurosis — A state of maladjustment (or mental illness) causing the person to show certain symptoms of mental disorder, yet these are not necessarily of such seriousness that the person is incapacitated, that is, unable to carry on his ordinary occupations.

NIMH — National Institute of Mental Health
Normalcy — This is the opposite of mental illness. Normal could mean,

under specified circumstances: 1. The average, (mathematical normal); 2. the ideal or perfectly healthy (desirable) state, and finally; 3. the ethical normal, or those actions which are in conformity with some set of moral principles.

Personality — That global quality which includes all the qualities of a person, whether on the conscious level or the unconscious, the rational or the vegetative, the voluntary or the involuntary. Simply it is the quality whereby a person is singular, unique, not fully like any other human being however similar he may be. Personality may be described either in terms of TYPES or of TRAITS or both. The emphasis here is always upon uniqueness or singularity. Finger-printing today gives us a good notion of this quality.

Personality Integration — The state in which the whole person acts in such a way that his output manifests good functioning on all levels of action and existence. Example: vegetative functions tie in with and support the sensory-motor, and both these contribute to harmonious functioning, under the direction of rationality both cognitive and volitional, whenever there is a complex situation involved.

Primariness — That quality which, according to the LeSenne-Berger scheme, inclines a person toward responding predominantly and spontaneously to immediate sensory impressions and stimulations. It is the opposite of secundarity.

Psychosis — A mental illness characterized by a rather complete break with reality. It may be chiefly a disturbance in the affective (emotional) sphere, or in the intellectual sphere or both. It usually results in inability to carry on one's regular occupations during the time that treatment is being applied.

Rationality — The capacity to use intelligence in all the ways possible (possessed only by human beings). These ways include abstracting an element common to many situations, making judgments about relationships, and comparing one relationship with another. In abnormal psychology the limits of rationality are discussed, namely those whereby a human being ceases to function normally as a rational human being, as in the case of a person during an epileptic seizure. Rationality implies that human beings act with awareness of what they are doing, and at least of some of the consequences of their acts. It presupposes the normal functioning of thought and volition, though these may be at a rather low ebb during states of semi-consciousness and diminished power of deliberation.

Secundarity — The trait whereby a person tends to react more readily in terms of past habit and persistent motivations. It is, for LeSenne-Berger, the opposite of primariness, and is also called perseveration. An example of mental perseveration would be persistent tunes running through one's head; one of motor perseveration would be continuing to tap one's foot according to the rhythm of a melody one has just heard.

Self-actuation — The making functional of any of man's latent powers or aptitudes, such as vision or memory or motor skills. The term **self** connotes that the activities in question are all attributable, in some sense at least, to one and the same total personality or **self**.

Self-ideal — The goal or goals one has in life, whether these be distant or immediate. More strictly the self-ideal, in this book, is taken to mean that kind of person or self, which each person strives or wants to become. In most cases this so-called ideal is far removed from the sphere of everyday choices and deliberations; it is largely habitual and spontaneous, or even deeply situated in the levels of unconscious of the individual.

Sociability — That quality of a person, whereby he inclines toward frequent close contacts and interactions with his fellow man, rather than the opposite. Countless paper-and-pencil tests for this quality, varying in scientific validity and reliability, may be found in any manual of tests of personality.

Stability — A quality whereby a person lacks frequent and unpredictable fluctuations in his total make-up, or in some aspect of his total personality. The extremely unstable person is not difficult to detect, even for the ordinary man of the street. The trait, as can be inferred very readily, is very relative. No one is or even can be perfectly stable in this life, in the mind of this writer.

Stress — A term used very widely in modern psychology, to signify in a person special kinds of distress, such as anxiety, depression, and such experiences as sorrows and loss of internal peace and harmony. The term is found most frequently in combination with **tolerance,** or rather with **frustration tolerance.** In the book it will be used in connection with discussions of **ego-strength.**

t test (Fischer — always used with a dash under the letter **t**) A measure which indicates the degree of significance attaching to the difference between two or more averages of two or more groups of persons; Example: Class 1A averages 91 and Class 1B 85 on a certain test. The **t** score (or critical ratio) tells one what the probability is that so great a difference will be obtained if another sample of students of the same kind are tested with the same test. Both **t** test and CR (critical ratio) are computed from the ratio that is found to exist in some pair of random samples, between the actual difference in averages for the two groups, and the standard error of this difference. Suitable formulae may be found in any elementary book on statistics.

Test Battery — A series of carefully prepared situations or tests, whose purpose is to give a rather complete picture (or profile) of a person's traits, aptitudes, and dispositions, without any attempt to evaluate them in terms of value.

Temperament — In America this term is usually taken to mean the emotional and mostly inherited part of the whole person. It is usually rather constant through life, and surely it is more invariant than either character or personality. An example would be the volatile and highly perseverant type who is quick to react and slow to recover, as opposed to the opposites.

Trait — Any quality of any person whereby this unique person may be distinguished quite well from any other one. Example: his finger-prints, or his sociability.

Type — A cluster of traits which may serve to distinguish a whole group of human beings from some other group. Example: The sociable type, the schizoid type, the manic type.

Type evaluation — Any estimate of the predominant temperamental and/or character-personality qualities of a person. It is stressed that an estimate made at one time in a person's life, is far from valid for some other period. This is because traits of character, personality and temperament have a way of modifying themselves during the life span of each and every individual.

Value — Any attribute whereby a thing may be said to be desirable, useful or good. The basis for the desirability may lie in the thing itself, such as food for sustenance; or in the pleasure which some use of it evokes, such as music or art; or finally in the inner quality itself, such as sanity, or health, or virtue for a human being. This last category of value requires the use of the rational powers of judgment and reasoning, in addition to the power of sense perception, in order to arrive at a typically human mode of evaluation.

BIBLIOGRAPHY*

Allport, Gordon, **The Individual and his Religion.** New York, Macmillan, 1950.

―――― **Personality: a psychological interpretation.** New York, H. Holt, 1960.

Cattel, R. B., **A Guide to Mental Testing.** U. of London Press, London E.C.4, 1936.

―――― **Personality.** New York, McGraw Hill, 1950.

Curran, C.A., **Counseling in Catholic Life and Education.** New York, Macmillan, 1952.

―――― **Personality Factors in Counseling.** New York, Grune and Stratton, 1945.

Devlin, W. J. (et. al.), **Psychodynamics of Personality Development.** Alba House, Staten Island, New York, 1964.

Dinello, F. A., An investigation of the influence of occupation on the Loyola Language Study. Unpublished Masters Thesis, Loyola University, Chicago, 1958.

Dittes, J. E., and Menges, R. J., **Psychological Studies of Clergymen: Abstracts of Research.** Thomas Nelson and Sons, New York, 1965.

Donceel, J. F., **The Philosophy of Human Nature.** 2nd Edition, New York, Sheed and Ward, 1961.

Ewalt, J. R. (M.D.), Second Annual Report, Joint Commission on Mental Health and Illness. Cambridge University Press, Massachusetts, 1957.

Frankl, Viktor, **From Death Camp to Existentialism.** New York, Basic Books Inc., 1958.

Gasson, John, **Philosophy and Unity.** Fifteenth Annual Convention of the JPA, Woodstock College Press, Woodstock, Maryland, 1953.

Gemelli, A., Ph.D., **Psychoanalysis Today.** New York, Kenedy, 1955.

Hagmaier, George, and Gleason, R. W., **Counseling the Catholic.** New York, Sheed and Ward, 1959.

Herr, V. V., "Mental Health Training in Catholic Seminaries," **Journal of Religion and Health,** January, 1962, pp. 127-152.

―――― Same title of article, same Journal, Vol. 5, No. 1, January, 1966, pp. 27-34.

―――― "The Loyola Language Study," **Journal of Clinical Psychology,** Vol. XIII, No. 3, 1957, pp. 258-262.

―――― Same Journal, Further Studies in the Loyola Language Study, Vol. XXII, No. 3, 1966, pp. 281-287.

Herr, V. V.; Arnold, M. G.; Weisgerber, Charles A.; D'Arcy, P. F., **Screening Candidates for the Priesthood and Religious Life.** The Loyola University Press, Chicago, 1964.

Herr, V. V., and Kobler, F. J., "Further Study of Psychogalvanometric Test for Neuroticism," **Journal of Clinical Psychology,** Vol. XIII, No. 4, pp.

―――――

* References in text and several books not cited.

387-390, 1957.
——— "A Psychogalvanometric Test for Neuroticism," **Journal of Abnormal and Soc. Psych.**, Vol. 48, No. 3, 1953.
Josselyn, I. M., **The Happy Child**. New York, Random House, 1955.
Jung, C. G., **Psychology of Types**. New York, Harcourt Brace, 1926.
Kronfeld., **Charakterkunde**. Stuttgart, 1936.
Kretschmer, E., **Physique and Character**. New York, Harcourt Brace, 1925.
Lazarus, R. S., Spiesman, J. C., Mordkoff, A. J., and Davison, L. A., "A Laboratory Study of Psychological Stress Produced by a Motion Picture Film," **Psychological Monographs, General and Applied**. No. 553, 1962.
Leo, M. (Brother), **Test of Temperament and Character**. Bulletin No. 12 (trans. from French); Institut Pedagogique Saint-Georges, U. of Montreal, Montreal, 1962.
Ligon, Ernst, **The Dimensions of Character**. New York, Macmillan, 1956.
Lucinia, Sister, A study of the relationship between communality of thought on the Loyola Language Study and empathic ability in Kerr's Empathy Test. Unpublished Master's Thesis, Loyola University, Chicago, 1966.
Maslow, A. H., **Religion, Values and Peak Experiences**. Columbus, Ohio, State University Press, 1964.
——— **Motivation and Personality**. New York, Harper and Bros., 1954.
Menges, R. J., and Dittes, J. E., **Psychological Studies of Clergymen: Abstracts of Research**. New York, Thomas Nelson and Sons, 1965.
Meissner, W. W., **Annotated Bibliography in Religion and Psychology**. New York, The Academy of Religion and Mental Health, 1961.
Montague, J. D., and Coles, E. M., "Mechanism and measurement of the galvanic skin response," **Psych. Bulletin**. Vol. 65, 1966, pp. 251-279.
Nuttin, Josef, **Psychoanalysis and Personality**. New York, Sheed and Ward, 1954.
O'Doherty, E. F. (M.A., Ph.D.) and McGrath, D. S. (R.R.C.P.I., D.P.M) eds., **The Priest and Mental Health**. Staten Island, New York, Alba House, 1963.
Outler, A. C., **Psychotherapy and the Christian Message**. New York, Harper and Bros., 1954.
Rogers, C. R., **Counseling and Psychotherapy**. New York, Houghton Mifflin, 1942.
——— **On Becoming a Person, A Therapist's View of Psychotherapy**. Boston, H. Mifflin, 1961.
Rosanoff, A. J., (M.D.) ed., **Manual of Psychiatry**. New York, John Wiley and Sons, 1927.
Royce, James, **Man and His Nature**. New York, McGraw Hill, 1961.
Schneiders, A. A., **Personal Adjustment and Mental Health**. New York, Rinehart, 1953.
Sheldon, W., **Varieties of Temperament**. New York, Harper, 1942.

Simoneaux, H. J., **Spiritual Guidance and Varieties of Character.** New York, Pageant Press, 1956.

Stagner, Ross, **Psychology of Personality,** 2nd Edition. New York, McGraw Hill, (1937) 1948.

Stephenson, W., "An introduction to so-called motor perseveration tests," **British J. Educ. Psychol.,** Vol. IV, 2, 1934, pp. 186-207.

Stewart, J. V. P., The reliability of the Loyola Language Study and its relation to values, interests, and group-mindedness. Unpublished doctoral dissertation, Loyola University, Chicago, 1963.

Strasser, S., **The Soul in Metaphysical and Empirical Psychology.** Pittsburgh, Duquesne University Press, 1957.

Thorne, F. C., "Principles of Personality Counseling, an eclectic viewpoint," **J. clin. Psychol.,** Brandon, Vt., 1950.

Thurstone, L. L., "Factorial Studies of Intelligence," **Psychometric Monographs** No. 2.

Vanderveldt, J. H., and Odenwald, R. P., **Psychiatry and Catholicism,** 2 nd Edition. New York McGraw Hill, 1957.

Walker, R. E., and Nicolay, R. C., (Nicolay is senior author), "Anxiety as a correlate of personal problems," **Psychological Reports,** 19, 53-54; Southern Universities Press, 1963.

Weisgerber, C. A., "Factor analysis of a questionnaire test on perseveration," **J. of Gen. Psych.** 53, 341-345, 1955.

———— "The relationship of perseveration to a number of personality traits and adjustment," **J. of Gen. Psych.** 50, 3-13, 1954.

———— "Conscious perseveration and persistence of Autonomic activity measured by recovery from the psychogalvanic response," **J. Gen. Psych.** 45, 83-93, 1951.

Welsh, G. S.; Dahlstrom, W. G., Minneapolis, **An MMPI Handbook: A guide to its use in clinical practice.** U. of Minn. Press, 1960. 1960.

Winer, N., **Statistical Principles in Experimental Design.** New York, McGraw Hill, 1962.

INDEX

Activity-inactivity, 36 ff.
Activity skill tendency, 36, 37
Adaptability, 101
Adjustment, 9 ff.
Adjustment, personal, 9, 10
Adjustment, social, 6, 10, 11
Aging, 4
Analysis of Variance: 98, 103 ff.
Analysis of Variance: Neurological tests, 8 ff., 104
Anxiety, external, 106
Anxiety, general (MAS), 103, 114
Anxiety, internal, 98
Anxiety, testing for 82, 87
Aptitude, 17
Attitude, 18

Basic conductance level, 93
Belonging, 10
Bibliography of Psychology and Religion, 142

California Mental Health Test, 9-11, 58
Cardinal Bea, 111
Cattell, R., 37, 57-58
Character, 2, 3, 13, 16-17, 31
Charity, 20, 24 ff.
Clergymen, and psychiatrists, 6-8
Comparing Collegians and Seminarians (CC&S): defensiveness, 101
  CC&S:LLS, 103 ff., 106, 108, 110 ff.
  CC&S: Neurological test, 101 ff.
  CC&S: Perseveration, 101, 106
Cooperation, 30
Counselling on basis of temperament tests, 51 ff.
Curran, Fr., 113

Defensiveness (K), 101
Depression, 65, 71
Devlin, Fr., 12
Discriminating seminarians, 78
Divine, 20, 62

Edwards Personal Audit, 58
Ego, 12, 23, 25
Eight Beatitudes, 26 ff.
Electrodermal responses (EDRs), momentary, 94 ff.
Emotional reactivity (Pd), 74 ff.
Emotionality (Pt), 74 ff., 81
Emotions, function of, 33, 63
Emotions, hygiene of, 34
Emotions, judging, 35, 69, 71
Emotivity, 33 ff., 41 ff., 57 ff., 71, 81
Empathy, See Loyola Language Study, 27
Environment, effect of, 15
Extraversion, 73 ff.
Ethics of using results, 79 ff.

Faith and Hope 23 ff.
Far Vision, 21
Free association, 83, 91, 92 ff.
Freedom from Nervous tendencies (Physical Symptoms), 11
  withdrawal tendencies (Sc), 11, 72, 76, 77, 78

Gestalt, 2
Goals, 20, 28

Haggard transformation, 95, 101-102
Hathaway, 72-73
Health, 3 ff., 29
Heymans and Wiersma, 32, 33, 40, 42
Humm-Wadsworth, 61

Hypochondriasis, 66, 72
Hypomania, 71, 74
Hysteria, 68, 75

Instructions, importance of, 107 ff.
Integration, 18 ff.
Intelligence, 17, 71, 84
Inventory (MMPI), 58, 65 ff.

"K" score, 90, 99 ff.
Knowledge, 14

Levels of Consciousness, 16, 99
Likelihood of Perseverance, 20
Loyola Battery, 119
Loyola Language Study (LLS), 88, 95 ff., 110
Loyola Services Center, 116

Magnaniminity, 28
Mental health, and religion, 6, 7, 24-25, 62, 126
and seminary training, 93
and society, 6, 23
signs of, 8 ff., 34
Mental health training of seminarians, 123, 124
Mental illness, signs of, 8, 9, 67, 68
Methods of analysis, 97 ff.
Minnesota Multiphasic Personality Inventory (MMPI), 58, 65, 88
Morality (moral behavior), 7, 52

National Institute of Mental Health, 123
Neurological Test, 88
Neuroticism, 90
Neuroticism test, partial, 96,
Neurotic index, 101, 109
Neurotic triad, 69 ff.
Normalcy, 28 ff., 88
Nouns, abstract & concrete, 1

Perseveration (retentivity), 39, 41, 42, 87, 98
and character, 39
and perseverance, 39
and PGR, 88
Stephenson's test of, 37
Personal inadequacy, 104, 114
Personal service, 13
Personal worth, 9, 21 ff., 31, 56, 62, 66
Personality, 12 ff.
Personality Assessment, 89
Personality integration, 18 ff.
Personality testing for religious candidates, 16, 73
Primeau, 111, 122
Psychasthenia, 66, 76
Psychological Studies of Clergymen, 86
Psychopathic deviate, 68
Psychosis, 68, 70
Purpose, 29

Rating and MMPI, 68 ff.
Rationality, 16
Reactivity emotional, 71
Rice-LaSenne-Berger, 33 ff., 38, 40, 51, 60, 109

Schizophrenia, 64, 92
Schenectady research, 27
Secondarity, 42
Self-actuation, 13 ff., 19, 24, 34, 65, 126
Self-fulfillment, 11, 18 ff., 22, 24 ff., 62
Self-ideal, 19 ff., 56
Self-rating, 108
Self-reliance, 9
Seminarians, and college males, 41, 62
Sex, and the psychiatrist, 7
Simoneaux, 32, 33, 59, 60

Sociability (MMPI), 85
Social introversion, 77
Stability, 20
Stephenson, W., 37
Stress, 96
Suspiciousness (Pa), 75 ff.
  Nervous, 41-42
  Phlegmatic, 42-43
  Sentimental, 43-45
  Sanguine, 45-46
  Choleric, 46-47
  Apathetic, 47-48
  Passionate, 48-49
  Amorphous, 49-50
  Affiinities and opposites, 50 ff.
  and avowed benefit from seminary training, 59, 64
  and psychiatric syndromes, 53, 57 ff.

Taylor Anxiety (Modified), 90, 107, 111
Team approach to selecting candidates, 80
Temperament, 2, 2, 13, 16, 31, 36, 50 ff., 60
Temperament tests, 37
Temperament types (TT), 31, 59 ff., 88,

Test Battery, evaluative, 90 ff., 110, 113 ff.
Thurstone's Neurotic Inventory, 58
Trait, 16, 19 ff., 31 ff., 54, 56
Trait-tendencies, 31 ff.
Trait classification, 32, 54 ff.
Trait complexes (TC), 42, 53, 58
  phlegmatic, 43
  sentimental, 44-45, 57
  sanguine, 46
  choleric, 47, 57
  apathetic, 48
  passionate, 49
  amorphous, 50
Type evaluation, 55 ff., 59 ff.
"Trigger" tendencies, 83

Validation, I, 3
Value, 14, 15, 35
Vatican Council on Seminary training, IX, 112 ff., 116
Volition 18,

Weisgerber's test, 38, 119
Will (Volition), 15, 18
Woodworth's Psychoneurotic Inventory, 58